Luke tells us the Good News about Jesus

Bible Society

Bible Society
Trinity Business Centre
Stonehill Green, Westlea
Swindon SN5 7DG
biblesociety.org.uk
bibleresources.org.uk

EasyEnglish Bible translation, copyright © 1997–2010 MissionAssist,
previously known as Wycliffe Associates (UK). This publication is in EasyEnglish
Level A (1200 words).

For permission to use excerpts of the EasyEnglish Bible translation please
contact MissionAssist, PO Box 257, Evesham WR11 9AW
Charity registration number 1007772
Visit: easyenglish.info

EasyEnglish Gospel of Luke
ISBN 978 0 564 04963 9

Typography and typesetting by Bible Society Resources Ltd,
a wholly-owned subsidary of The British and Foreign Bible Society
Cover design by Patrick Knowles
Production arranged by Bible Society Resources Ltd

EEGLUK/BSRL/2022/0.25M
Printed in the United Kingdom

CONTENTS

Luke tells us the Good News about Jesus

A word list at the end explains words with a star* by them

About this book

Luke obeyed what Jesus taught. He was also a doctor. People think that he was not a Jew*. He wrote this book some time between the years AD* 59 and AD* 80. Some people think that he wrote it in the city called Rome. He wrote it for a man called Theophilus. He was an important Roman* officer and he was a rich man.

Luke also wrote the book for other people that believed in Jesus. It would help them to know Jesus better. Then they could answer questions when people asked them about him. Many people had wrong ideas about Jesus. Luke wanted people to know what was true.

Luke writes about the Good News. The Good News is that God wants to rule in the lives of his people. God will rule in the lives of Jews* and of those people that are not Jews*. Luke tells us who Jesus is. And he tells us how Jesus was born. He also tells us about his life and death. Luke explains to us why Jesus came to earth. He also explains what he did during his life here. And he tells us how he went to live with God again. And, at the end, he explains to us about God's gift of the Holy Spirit*.

Luke knew that Jesus had told people about the Good News. Jesus wanted his people to let everyone in the world know the message about himself. Luke wanted everyone to know what Jesus had said.

The book of Luke is in 4 parts:

1. What happened before Jesus started his work (1:1 - 4:13).
2. What happened when Jesus was working in the country called Galilee (4:14 - 9:50).
3. What happened when Jesus was working in the countries called Judea and Perea (9:51 - 19:27).
4. What happened in the city called Jerusalem in the last week of Jesus' life (19:28 - 24:53).

LUKE

1

¹Great things have happened in our country. Many people have tried to write about them. ²Some people were present when these things started to happen. They saw everything that happened. They told us what they had seen. And they told us what they had heard. They are the people who told the Good News. ³Most important Theophilus, I have checked all these facts. Now I also know about all the things that happened from the beginning. I am writing to tell them to you. It is good for you also to know all these facts. This is the reason for this letter. ⁴You have already heard about all these things. Now you can be sure that they are true.

What happened before John the Baptist* was born

⁵ There was a man whose name was Zechariah. He lived when Herod was king of Judea. Zechariah was a priest* and he belonged to a group of priests* from the family* of Abijah. He had a wife called Elizabeth. And they were both from the family* of the priest* called Aaron.

⁶Zechariah and Elizabeth obeyed God all the time. They did not do wrong things. God liked how they lived. ⁷But they had no children. Elizabeth could not have a baby and they were both getting old.

⁸One day, Zechariah's group was working at the Great House of God*. And Zechariah had a special job to do. ⁹The priests* chose one of their group to go into a special room inside the Great House of God*. Zechariah's job was to burn incense* there.

¹⁰While Zechariah was burning incense*, many men were outside the special room. They were praying to God.

¹¹The incense* was burning on a special table, when an angel* from God appeared to Zechariah. The angel* was standing at the right hand side of the table.

¹² When Zechariah saw the angel*, he was very surprised. He was also very afraid. ¹³'Zechariah, do not be afraid', the angel* said to him. 'God has heard what you prayed. He will give you what you asked for. Your wife Elizabeth will have a baby boy. You will call him John. ¹⁴⁻¹⁵He will be very important to the LORD. So, he will make you very happy. Many other people will also be very happy because he has been born. He must never drink anything with alcohol in it. From the time that he is born, the Holy Spirit* will live inside him.

¹⁶He will teach many people in Israel*. Then they will turn their lives towards the LORD their God and they will obey God again. ¹⁷John will prepare the people for the LORD. The Holy Spirit* will lead John as he led Elijah. John will be as powerful as Elijah was. He will help fathers to love their children. He will teach people that do not obey God. Then they will think right things. And they will do right things that good people do. John will prepare Israel's* people. Then they will be ready when the LORD comes.'

¹⁸'How can I be sure about this?' Zechariah asked the angel*. 'After all, I am an old man. My wife is also old.'

¹⁹'I am called Gabriel', answered the angel*. 'My place is in front of God. I am always ready to work for God. He has sent me to speak to you. He told me that I should tell you this good news. ²⁰Now listen to me. Because you did not believe my message, you will be quiet. You will not speak again until the time that your son is born. My message will become true at the right time.'

²¹While this was happening, the people outside were waiting for Zechariah. They were thinking, 'Why has Zechariah stayed

for such a long time in the special room? Why has he not come out yet?' ²²When he did come out, he tried to talk to them. But he could not speak. So they knew that he had seen something special in the room. He was moving his head and his hands about, to tell them what had happened. But he remained quiet.

²³When Zechariah had finished his work in the Great House of God*, he returned home. ²⁴Soon, a baby was growing inside his wife Elizabeth. She stayed in her house for 5 months. ²⁵'The LORD has now given me a baby', she said. 'He has been kind to me. He has helped me to feel good about myself. Because of this, other people cannot say bad things about me any longer.'

What happened before Jesus was born

²⁶When Elizabeth's baby had grown inside her for nearly 6 months, God sent the angel* Gabriel to Nazareth. Nazareth is a town in Galilee. ²⁷Gabriel went there to visit a young woman. Her name was Mary. She had never had sex with anyone. She had promised to marry a man called Joseph. He belonged to the family* of King David.

²⁸Gabriel arrived. 'Hello, Mary', he said. 'God loves you very much. He is very near to you.'

²⁹Mary had a lot of problems in her mind about what Gabriel said. She did not understand why he said it. ³⁰'Do not be afraid, Mary', Gabriel went on to say. 'God has been kind to you. ³¹Listen! A baby boy will grow inside you. When he is born, you will call him Jesus. ³²He will be great. The strong God above will call him his Son. The LORD God will make him king. He will rule as King David ruled. ³³He will rule over the family* of Jacob for all time. He will be king for all time.'

³⁴'How can this happen?' Mary asked. 'I have never had sex with anyone.' ³⁵'The Holy Spirit* will come to you', the angel* answered. 'The power of God will cover you like a shadow. So, your child will be completely good. He will never do anything that is wrong. He will be called God's Son. ³⁶Another thing! Your cousin, Elizabeth, is very old. People said that she could not have a baby. Listen! She

also will have a son. The baby has grown inside her now for nearly 6 months. 37There is nothing that God cannot do.'

38 'I am the servant of the LORD', Mary answered. 'I have heard what you have said. I want the LORD to cause it to happen to me.' Then the angel* left her.

Mary visits Elizabeth

39 After that, Mary prepared herself and she left on a journey. She hurried to a town in the hills of Judea. 40When she arrived at the home of Zechariah, she said, 'Hello' to Elizabeth. 41When Elizabeth heard Mary speak, she felt her baby move quickly inside her. The Holy Spirit* filled her. 42Then she spoke to Mary in a loud voice, 'God has made you very happy. He has been more good and kind to you than to other women. He has also been good and kind to your baby. 43I am not an important person and you are the mother of my LORD. So, it is a very good thing that you have visited me. 44Listen! When I heard you say, "Hello" to me, the baby moved quickly inside me. He was very happy. 45The LORD told you what would happen. And you believed what he told you. This makes you a very happy person.'

This is Mary's song

46Then Mary said,

'All of me wants to say to the LORD, "How good and great you are!"
47I am happy because of God. It is he who saves me.
48 I do not think that I am an important person.
God knows this, so he has looked at me with love.
Listen! From now on all people will say that
God has been very good and kind to me.
49After all, God has done great things for me.
He is very powerful and strong.
He is good in everything.
50He is kind to people that obey him.

He is also kind to all their children. He will do this for
all time.
51 He has shown how strong he is.
Some people think that they are very important.
But he has sent them away alone in different directions.
52 Some people were ruling countries.
But he has taken their important jobs away from them.
He has given important work to people that do not
feel important.
53 He has fed hungry people with good things.
He has sent rich people away with nothing.
54 He promised that he would never forget his people, Israel*.
Now he has helped them.
55 He made a promise to Abraham and to our other fathers*.
"I will be kind to you for all time", he said. Now he has done
what he promised.'

56 Mary stayed with Elizabeth for about three months. Then
she returned to her home.

John the Baptist* is born

57 Then it was time for Elizabeth to have her baby. She had a
son. 58 Her family and the people that lived near her heard
about her baby. They knew that the LORD had been very kind
to her. They saw that she was happy. So they were happy too.
59 When the child was 8 days old, they came to the house of
Zechariah and Elizabeth. The child had to be circumcised* on
that day. The people wanted to call the child Zechariah. This
was the same name that his father had.

60 'No', said Elizabeth. 'His name will be John.'

61 'You cannot really want his name to be John!' they said. 'You
do not have anybody in your family called John.' 62 Then they
moved their hands at his father. They wanted to know the
boy's name.

63 So Zechariah asked for something to write on. He wrote, 'His
name is John.' Everyone was very surprised at what he wrote.

⁶⁴Immediately, Zechariah could speak again. He could speak very well again. He began to tell God, 'You are very great!'

⁶⁵The people that lived near Zechariah and Elizabeth were surprised. They were surprised about what had happened. They saw how great God was. Many people that lived in the hills of Judea also talked about all these things. ⁶⁶Everyone that heard about these things thought about them. 'What will this child be?' they asked each other. After all, they could see that God really was with him.

This is Zechariah's song

⁶⁷The Holy Spirit* filled John's father. Then he spoke well about God. The Holy Spirit* helped him to speak this message.

⁶⁸'The LORD God of Israel* is a great God.
He has come to save his people.
⁶⁹He has sent a very strong person that will save us.
This person is in the family* of David. David was his servant.
⁷⁰Long ago, God gave his Spirit to good people so that they could tell us about this.
This is what they said:
⁷¹"God will save us from our enemies.
He will save us from everyone that hates* us.
⁷²He has promised to be kind to our fathers*.
He will remember to do the things that he promised."
⁷³Yes, he will remember the promises that he said
to Abraham.'
⁷⁴' "I will keep you safe from your enemies.
Then you can work for me and not be afraid.
⁷⁵You can work for me in the right way.
You can do this all your lives." '
⁷⁶Zechariah then spoke to his child.
'You, child, will be called a servant of the great God above.
The Holy Spirit* will give to you messages to speak.
You will go in front of the LORD to prepare a way for him.
⁷⁷You will tell his people how God can save them.

They have done wrong things but God will forgive* them.
78 Our God will forgive* us because he is very kind.
He will send someone from the highest place.
This person will be like the sunrise to us.
79 As the sun gives light to everybody, so he will shine on all people.
Some people are like people who are in the dark.
They are living without God.
Some people are afraid to die.
But he will shine on everybody.
He will show us how to live so that we will not be afraid.'

80 Zechariah's child grew. God made him strong in his mind. He went and he lived in the desert* for many years. Later, God sent him to Israel's* people, to teach them.

2

Jesus is born

1 While Mary's baby was growing inside her, Caesar Augustus was ruling the whole Roman* world. He ordered* his men, 'Count everyone who is in the Roman* world.' 2 This was the first time that the Romans* had counted everyone. Quirinius was the Roman* ruler of Syria at this time.

3 So everyone went to his own home town for the Romans* to count them. 4 Joseph also went to his home town. He was living in the town called Nazareth in Galilee. He went to the town called Bethlehem in Judea. King David had been born there, so Bethlehem was called the town of David. Joseph belonged to the family* of David. That is why he went to Bethlehem.

5 Joseph took Mary with him so that the Romans* could count them. She went because she had promised to marry him. She would soon have a baby.

6 While they were in Bethlehem, her baby was born. 7 This was her first baby, and it was a boy. She put cloths round him. Then

she put him in an animal's feeding box. She did this because they could not stay in the hotel. There were no empty rooms for them.

Some people leave their sheep to go and see Jesus

8 That night some people were living in the fields near Bethlehem. They were keeping their sheep safe. 9 Then an angel* of the Lord appeared to them. A bright light from God shone all round them. So that frightened them very much. 10 'Do not be afraid', the angel* said. 'Listen! I bring you good news. This news will make everyone very happy. 11 Something happened today in the town of David. Someone special was born. It is he who will save you. He is the Messiah*. He is the Lord. 12 I will tell you how you will know this baby. You will find him with cloths round him. He is lying in an animal's feeding box.'

13 Just then a lot more angels* also appeared. They were speaking about God.

14 'God is beautiful and great and important', they said.

'He lives in the highest place.

He will be good to the people on earth that make him happy.

They will not have troubles in their minds or in their spirits*.'

15 After that, the angels* returned to God's home. Then these people said to each other, 'Perhaps we should leave the sheep and go to Bethlehem immediately! The Lord has sent angels* to tell us what has happened. We want to see this baby.'

16 So they hurried to Bethlehem. There, they found Mary and Joseph with the baby. The baby really was lying in a feeding box. 17 After they had seen the baby, they told everybody about him. They told them what the angel* had said to them. 18 Many people heard what the men said. They were very surprised. 19 Mary remembered all that the men from the fields had said. She thought about everything for a long time. 20 The men then returned to their sheep. 'How great you are!' they were saying

to God. 'How good you are! Everything that the angel* told us was true! We have heard good news. We have seen very special things!'

Mary and Joseph take Jesus to the Great House of God*

21 When the baby was 8 days old, it was time for the priest* to circumcise* him. His parents called him Jesus. The angel* had told Mary that she must call the baby, Jesus. He told her that before she had a baby inside her.

22 Long ago, the LORD gave Moses rules for his people to obey. One rule told how to become clean* after a baby was born. Now the time had come for Mary and Joseph to obey this rule. So, they took the baby Jesus to the Great House of God* in Jerusalem to show him to the LORD.

23 This is what the LORD had said: 'The first male baby born to a woman or to an animal is mine. So you must bring him to me. 24 When you do this, also bring two special birds for the priest* to kill.' That is what Mary and Joseph did.

25 At this time, a man called Simeon was living in Jerusalem. He was good and he always obeyed God. He had waited a long time to see the special person that would save Israel*. The Holy Spirit* was with Simeon. 26 'You will not die yet', the Holy Spirit* had told him. 'You know that God has promised to send the Messiah*. You will see him before you die.' 27 Now the day had come. The Holy Spirit* told Simeon that he should go to the Great House of God*. Mary and Joseph were bringing the baby Jesus to do what the rule said. 28 Simeon went to them. He took Jesus from Mary and he held him in his arms. Then he thanked God.

29 'Master, you have done what you promised to your servant. Now, I can die with no trouble in my mind.

30 Now I really have seen the person that will save people.

31 You have sent him to earth so that everyone will know about him.

32 He will be like a light to people. He will show you to those that are not Jews*. They will then know you. And they will know what you want from them. Then they will know what you want them to do. He will also show that your people of Israel* are very special.'

33 That is what Simeon said about Jesus. His message surprised Mary and Joseph very much.

34 Then Simeon asked God to be good and kind to Mary and to Joseph. After that, he spoke just to Mary, the mother of Jesus. 'God has chosen this baby. Many people in Israel* will become less important because of him. And many people will become alive again because of him. He will be like a sign that points to God. Many people will speak against him. 35 This will show their secret thoughts about God. This will make you very sad, too. It will seem that a sharp knife is cutting inside you. That is how sad you will be', Simeon said to her.

36 A very old lady called Anna was there in the Great House of God*, too. She often spoke messages that the Holy Spirit* gave to her. She was the daughter of Phanuel. She belonged to the family* of Asher. She had lived with her husband for 7 years and then he had died.

37 After that, she had lived alone until she was 84 years old. Now she never left the Great House of God*. She stayed there day and night to pray to God. Often she went without food so that she could pray better.

38 At that moment, Anna came to where Mary and Joseph were standing. When Anna saw the baby, she began to thank God for him. Then she began to speak about him to other people. Many people were waiting for God to make Jerusalem free*. These were the people that she was speaking to.

39 When Mary and Joseph had finished obeying all the rules, they returned home. They went back to the town called Nazareth in Galilee. 40 There the child grew. God was good

and kind to him and God made him strong. He could then understand many things.

The boy Jesus visits the Great House of God*

41 Every year, Mary and Joseph went to Jerusalem for the Passover* week.

42 When Jesus was 12 years old, his parents took him with them to Jerusalem. They went as usual for the Passover* week. 43 When the week finished, everyone left to return home. The boy Jesus stayed behind in Jerusalem, but his parents did not know this. 44 They thought that he was with their group. So they travelled for a whole day. Then they began to look for him among their family and friends.

45 They could not find him, so they went back to Jerusalem. They looked for him for three days, 46 before they found him in the Great House of God*. He was sitting among the teachers. He was listening to what they were saying. He was also asking them questions. 47 Everyone that was listening to Jesus was very surprised. He understood so many things and he could answer difficult questions. 48 When his parents saw him there, they were also very surprised. 'My son', said his mother, 'why have you done this to us? Your father and I have looked everywhere for you. We have had a lot of troubles in our mind.'

49 'You should not really have had to look for me', Jesus answered. 'I must be doing what my Father wants me to do. Really, you should have known that.' 50 But they did not really understand what he was saying to them.

51 Jesus returned to Nazareth with them and he obeyed them. Mary was careful to remember all the special things that had happened. She thought about them a lot. 52 Jesus grew into a man. He could understand more and more things. Everyone loved him and God also thought well of him.

3

John the Baptist* prepares people to welcome Jesus

¹ This report about John, the son of Zechariah, began while
Tiberius Caesar was ruling the Roman* world. He had ruled for
almost 15 years. Pontius Pilate was ruling the country called
Judea. And Herod was ruling the land called Galilee. Philip
was the brother of Herod. He was ruling the countries called
Iturea and Traconitis. Lysanias was ruling Abilene. ²While
these men were ruling, the most important priests* were
Annas and Caiaphas. At that time John, the son of Zechariah,
was living in the desert*. He heard God speak to him.

³ John travelled to many places near to the river Jordan. 'You
are doing many bad things', he taught everybody. 'Stop doing
them. You should be sorry for what you have done. If you are,
I will baptise* you with water. God will then forgive* you.'

⁴John was teaching as Isaiah had spoken a long time before.
God gave him messages. Someone wrote down these messages
in a book. Isaiah told people what would happen. He said:

'People will hear someone who is shouting in the desert*:
"The LORD is coming.
Make the road ready for him.
Make it straight.
⁵ Fill in every valley and make every mountain and hill flat.
Take away every curve so that the road is straight.
Take away all the rocks so that the road is flat.
⁶ Then you will see how God will save you." '

⁷ Crowds of people were coming out into the desert* to hear
John speak. They wanted John to baptise* them. 'Yes', he said,
'God will soon punish* people that do wrong things. But you
are as dangerous as snakes. ⁸You have to show that you are
sorry. You have to show it by how you live. Stop doing things
that God does not like. Do not begin to say to yourselves, "God

will not punish* us. After all, we are part of the family* of Abraham." Listen! God can make children for Abraham out of these stones! ⁹You are like trees that have bad fruit. People cut down bad trees and they throw them into the fire. In the same way*, God will punish* bad people. And he will do it very soon.'

¹⁰'So, what should we do?' the crowd asked.

¹¹'If you have two shirts, give one away. Give it to a man that does not have a shirt. If you have some food, give some of it away. Give some to a man that has no food.'

¹²In the crowd, there were people that took money on behalf of the government. These men also wanted John to baptise* them. 'Teacher, what should we do?' they asked. ¹³'You must take the right amount of money from the people. You must not take more than the rules say.'

¹⁴Then some soldiers spoke. 'What about us? What should we do?'

'Do not rob people of their money', John replied. 'Do not say that a person has done something wrong, if he has not. It is wrong to get money by doing that. And you must be happy with the money that you get for your work.'

¹⁵'Is John the Messiah*?' the people were thinking. 'Is he the man that God will send to save Israel*?' They were all hoping that he might be. ¹⁶John knew what they were thinking. 'I have only baptised* you with water', he said. 'But someone else is coming to baptise* people. He is much greater and more important than I am. He is so important that I am not good enough even to undo his shoes. He will baptise* some of you with the Holy Spirit* and with fire. ¹⁷Think about a farmer that brings the wheat* home. Then he uses a tool to make the seeds separate from what remains. He stores all the seeds. But he burns all that remained. This person will be like that. He will come very soon. He will keep good people safe. But he will punish* bad people in the fire that nobody can put out.'

¹⁸John said many more things to the people. He was telling them the good news about how God could change their lives. ¹⁹But the ruler Herod stopped him. John had told Herod that it was wrong for him to marry Herodias. She was the wife of his brother. John had also told Herod that he had done many other bad things.

²⁰Then Herod did an even worse thing; he locked John up in prison.

John baptises* Jesus

²¹While John was baptising* all the people, he also baptised* Jesus. When Jesus was praying, the sky opened. ²²Then the Holy Spirit* came down. He seemed like a bird. He came and he rested on Jesus. People heard a voice from the sky. 'You are my Son. I love you. You make me very happy.'

The family* of Jesus

²³Jesus was about 30 years old when he started to tell the Good News. People thought that he was the son of Joseph.
He was from the family of Heli.
²⁴ Heli was from the family of Matthat.
Matthat was from the family of Levi.
Levi was from the family of Melchi.
Melchi was from the family of Jannai.
Jannai was from the family of Joseph.
²⁵ Joseph was from the family of Mattathias.
Mattathias was from the family of Amos.
Amos was from the family of Nahum.
Nahum was from the family of Esli.
Esli was from the family of Naggai.
²⁶ Naggai was from the family of Maath.
Maath was from the family of Mattathias.
Mattathias was from the family of Semein.
Semein was from the family of Josech.
Josech was from the family of Joda.
²⁷ Joda was from the family of Joanan.

Joanan was from the family of Rhesa.
Rhesa was from the family of Zerubbabel.
Zerubbabel was from the family of Shealtiel.
Shealtiel was from the family of Neri.
28 Neri was from the family of Melchi.
Melchi was from the family of Addi.
Addi was from the family of Cosam.
Cosam was from the family of Elmadam.
Elmadam was from the family of Er.
29 Er was from the family of Joshua.
Joshua was from the family of Eliezer.
Eliezer was from the family of Jorim.
Jorim was from the family of Matthat.
Matthat was from the family of Levi.
30 Levi was from the family of Simeon.
Simeon was from the family of Judah.
Judah was from the family of Joseph.
Joseph was from the family of Jonam.
Jonam was from the family of Eliakim.
31 Eliakim was from the family of Melea.
Melea was from the family of Menna.
Menna was from the family of Mattatha.
Mattatha was from the family of Nathan.
Nathan was from the family of David.
32 David was from the family of Jesse.
Jesse was from the family of Obed.
Obed was from the family of Boaz.
Boaz was from the family of Salmon.
Salmon was from the family of Nahshon.
33 Nahshon was from the family of Amminadab.
Amminadab was from the family of Ram.
Ram was from the family of Hezron.
Hezron was from the family of Perez.
Perez was from the family of Judah.
34 Judah was from the family of Jacob.
Jacob was from the family of Isaac.
Isaac was from the family of Abraham.

Abraham was from the family of Terah.
Terah was from the family of Nahor.
35 Nahor was from the family of Serug.
Serug was from the family of Reu.
Reu was from the family of Peleg.
Peleg was from the family of Eber.
Eber was from the family of Shelah.
36 Shelah was from the family of Cainan.
Cainan was from the family of Arphaxad.
Arphaxad was from the family of Shem.
Shem was from the family of Noah.
Noah was from the family of Lamech.
37 Lamech was from the family of Methuselah.
Methuselah was from the family of Enoch.
Enoch was from the family of Jared.
Jared was from the family of Mahalaleel.
Mahalaleel was from the family of Cainan.
38 Cainan was from the family of Enosh.
Enosh was from the family of Seth.
Seth was from the family of Adam.
Adam was from God.

4

The devil* tries to cause Jesus to do wrong things

1 Jesus was now full of the Holy Spirit*. When he returned from the river Jordan, the Holy Spirit* led him into the desert*. 2 He stayed there for 40 days and he did not eat anything. At the end of 40 days, he was very hungry. During this time the devil* tried to cause Jesus to do wrong things. They were things that God did not want him to do.

3 'If you are the Son of God*', the devil* said, 'change this stone into food.'

4 'No!' Jesus replied, 'the book of God says that food alone cannot cause people to live.'

⁵ After that, the devil* led Jesus up to a high place. In one moment, he showed him all the countries in the whole world. ⁶'I will let you rule the whole world', the devil* said, 'and I will give you power over everyone and over everything. It all belongs to me. So, I can give it to anyone that I choose. ⁷Just bend your knee in front of me. And say that I am great and important. Then I will give you the whole world to rule over.'

⁸'No!' Jesus replied. 'This is what God says in his book:

> "Bend your knee in front of the Lᴏʀᴅ God. Tell him how great and important he is. Only obey him." '

⁹ The devil* now took Jesus to Jerusalem. He led him to the highest part of the Great House of God*. Then he said, 'If you are the Son of God*, jump down from here to the ground. ¹⁰After all, it says in God's book:

> "God will order* his angels* to keep you safe."

¹¹ It also says,

> "They will hold you safe in their hands. They will not let you hurt your feet against a stone." '

¹²'No!' replied Jesus. 'That is not what God wants. His book says,

> "Do not do something dangerous just to cause God to save you." '

¹³The devil* tried to cause Jesus to do many things that God did not like. When the devil* had finished, he left Jesus alone for a time.

Jesus goes to Nazareth

¹⁴The Holy Spirit* continued to make Jesus very powerful when he returned to Galilee. Everyone who lived in and near

Galilee heard the news about him. 15 He taught in the Jewish*
meeting places and everyone said good things about him.

16 Jesus came to Nazareth, the town where he had grown up.
On the Jewish* day for rest, he went into the meeting place.
He always did this. Then he stood up to read aloud from the
Old Testament*.

17 They gave him the book of messages that God had given
to Isaiah. Jesus opened the book. He found the place where
Isaiah wrote.

> 18 'The Spirit from the LORD God is upon me.
> He has chosen me to tell good news to poor people.
> He has sent me to tell people who are in prison, "You can go
> free*!"
> I must say to people that cannot see, "See again!"
> I must cause people that are like slaves to be free*.
> 19 I must tell everyone, "This is the year when God will save
> his people." '

20 Jesus closed the book and he gave it back to an officer of
the meeting place. Then he sat down to teach the people.
Everyone in the meeting place was looking at him.

21 'Today', Jesus said to them, 'this message has become true.
It has happened while you were listening.'

22 Everyone was saying good things about Jesus. They were
surprised. 'How well he spoke! And he is only the son of
Joseph, is he not?' they were asking each other.

23 'Next', Jesus replied, 'you will be repeating the proverb*,
"Doctor, make people well in your own town." We have heard
that you did many surprising things in Capernaum. This is your
home town, so do the same things here! 24 People do not accept
a person that comes from their home town. That really is true.
They do not believe that he receives messages from God.

25 What I shall tell you now is true. Elijah received messages
from God. Elijah said that it would stop raining. And it did not

rain for three and a half years. So there was no food or water to drink in all the country. There were many widows* in the country of Israel* at that time. 26 But God did not send Elijah to stay with a widow* in Israel*. Instead, God sent Elijah to the country called Sidon. There Elijah stayed with a widow* in a place called Zarephath.'

27 'Here is another example. There were many people in Israel* with bad illnesses of the skin, when God's servant Elisha was alive. But God did not make any of them well. Instead, he made a man from the country called Syria well. The man was called Naaman.'

28 The people in the meeting place heard what Jesus said. They became very angry. 29 They stood up and they caused him to leave the town. The town was on the top of a hill. So, they took him to the top and they wanted to throw him down. 30 But Jesus walked through the middle of the crowd and he went away.

Jesus causes a bad spirit* to leave a man

31 Jesus went down to a town in Galilee called Capernaum. On the Jewish* day for rest, he began to teach in the meeting place. 32 They were really surprised because his words had authority. 33 In the meeting place was a sick man. He had a bad spirit* that was living inside him. The spirit* caused him to shout and to make a lot of noise. 34 'Jesus of Nazareth, what do you want to do to us? Have you come to destroy us? I know who you are. You are the Holy One*. You come from God.'

35 'Be quiet!' Jesus replied. 'Come out of the man.' At this, the bad spirit* caused the man to fall to the ground in front of the people. Then it came out without hurting him.

36 All the people were very surprised and they said to each other, 'How can this man speak in that way*? He has power and authority. When he orders* bad spirits* to come out of people, they come out.' 37 Then they began to tell everyone

about Jesus. As a result, people in all the places near Capernaum heard the news about Jesus.

Jesus makes many people well

38 Jesus then left the meeting place and he went into Simon's home. The mother of Simon's wife was sick with a very bad fever*. So, they asked Jesus to make her well. 39 Jesus came and he stood near her. He then ordered* the fever* to go away and it left her. So, she got up immediately and she began to prepare food for her visitors.

40 When the sun began to go down, the people brought many sick people to see Jesus. They had many different illnesses. He put his hands on each person and they became well.

41 Bad spirits* also came out of many people. The spirits* knew that he was the Messiah*. So, when they came out, they began to shout, 'Jesus, you are the Son of God*.' But Jesus stopped them shouting. He would not let them speak.

42 Early the next morning, Jesus went alone to a quiet place. The people went to look for him. When they found him they said, 'Do not leave us! Please stay with us in Capernaum.' 43 'I cannot stay with you', Jesus replied. 'I must go to other towns to teach everyone the good news. I will tell them how God rules in the lives of his people. That is what God sent me to do.'

44 Then he left them. And he started to teach in other Jewish* meeting places in the country called Judea.

5

Jesus asks some men to follow him

1 One day, Jesus was standing on the shore of Lake Gennesaret. And a crowd was pushing to get near to him. They were listening to him. He was talking about the message of God.

² Jesus saw two fishing boats at the edge of the lake. The fishermen* had left the boats there and they were now washing their nets*.

³ One of the boats was Simon's. So Jesus climbed into it. He then asked Simon to push it away a little from the shore. When Jesus had sat down in the boat, he started to teach the people again.

⁴ When he finished teaching them, he spoke to Simon. 'Now take the boat out into deep water', he said. 'Then put down the nets* into the water to catch some fish.'

⁵ 'Teacher', Simon replied, 'we worked all last night and we did not catch anything. But because you say it, I will put down the nets*.' ⁶ So they went and they put the nets* down into the water. When they did that, they caught many fish. There were so many fish that the nets* began to break. ⁷ So Simon shouted to the other fishermen* that always worked with him. 'Come', he said, 'we need you.' When they saw that, the men came in their boat. They filled both boats with the fish. There were so many that the boats began to go down. ⁸ When Simon saw all the fish, he went down on his knees in front of Jesus. He was afraid. 'Sir', he said, 'I am a bad man. So please leave me.'

⁹ Simon said this because he was very surprised. He was surprised because they had caught so many fish. His friends in the other boat were very surprised, too. ¹⁰ James and John were also very surprised. They were sons of Zebedee and they always worked with Simon. 'Do not be afraid of me', Jesus then said to Simon. 'From now on you will catch men!'

¹¹ After that, they went and they pulled their boats up on the shore. Then they left everything and they went with Jesus.

This is about a man with an illness of his skin and bones

¹² One day, Jesus was in a certain town. A man with an illness of his skin and bones that was called leprosy was there.

13 Jesus touched him with his hand. 'I do want to', he said. 'Be well.' Immediately, the illness was gone. 14 'Do not tell anyone about this', Jesus said to him. 'Instead, go and show yourself to the priest*. Take him a gift for God. Moses told people, "You must do this when you are better from this illness." So give this gift to God. This will show everyone that you are now well.'

15 After this, more and more people started to hear the news about Jesus. Crowds were coming to hear him teach. The sick ones also wanted him to make them well. 16 But he would go away from the crowd to pray in quiet places.

Jesus makes well a man that cannot walk

17 One day, while Jesus was teaching in a house, many people were sitting there. Some were Pharisees*. Other people were teachers of God's rules. They had come from many villages in Galilee, and from Judea and Jerusalem. At that time, the power of the LORD was present for Jesus to make sick people well.

18 Then some men arrived. They were carrying a man on a small carpet. The man could not move his legs. They tried to get into the house, because they wanted to bring the man to Jesus. 19 But the house was full of people, and they could not get in. So, they carried the small carpet with the man on it to the flat roof of the house. Then they made a hole in the roof. After that, they put the small carpet down through the hole. The man was still lying on it. He came down in the middle of the crowd, in front of Jesus. 20 When Jesus saw this, he said to himself, 'These men really believe in me.' So, he spoke to the sick man. 'My friend', he said. 'I forgive* you for all the bad things that you have done.'

21 The Pharisees* and the teachers of God's rules were there. They heard what Jesus said. So, they began to talk to each other about it. 'What he says is wrong. He cannot forgive* people for the things that they have done. Only God can do that. And he is only a man.' 22 Jesus knew what these men

were saying. 'You should not be thinking these things', he told them. ²³'I said to this man, "I forgive* you for all the bad things that you have done." But I could say to him, "Get up and walk." I want to show you that my words are true. Which is the best one to say? ²⁴Now I will show you that I, the Son of Man*, have authority on earth. I can forgive* people for the bad things that they have done. I will show you that I can forgive them.' Then he turned to the man that could not move his legs. 'I say to you', he said, 'stand up. Take up your carpet and go home!'

²⁵Immediately, the man stood up in front of them. He took the carpet that he had used to lie on. He went home. 'How great and powerful God is', he was saying. ²⁶What had happened surprised everyone. They were afraid. 'How great and powerful God is', they said to each other. 'We have seen very strange and special things happen today.'

Jesus asks Levi to come with him

²⁷After this happened, Jesus went for a walk. He saw a man that took money on behalf of the government. His name was Levi and he was working in his office. 'Follow me', Jesus said to him. ²⁸Levi got up and followed him. He left everything behind.

²⁹Soon after this, Levi made a large meal for Jesus at his house. A big crowd of people also came and they were eating with them. Many of these people also took money on behalf of the government. ³⁰Some Pharisees* and teachers of God's rules saw them. They did not like these people. So, they spoke to the men that followed Jesus. 'You eat and drink with these bad people. That is not right. Some of them even take money on behalf of the government.'

³¹'People that are well do not need a doctor', Jesus answered them. 'It is sick people that need one. ³²I have not come for people that have not done wrong things. Some people know that they have done wrong things. I am asking those people to

come to me. I want them to stop doing wrong things. I want them to start doing right things.'

33 When they heard this, they asked Jesus about something else. 'Some people obey what John the Baptist* teaches. Those people often stop eating food to pray better. The people that obey the Pharisees* do the same. Why do those that obey you never go without their meals?'

34 Jesus used a picture story to answer their question. 'When a man is marrying, he gives a big meal. His friends do not go without food then. 35 But the time will come when people will take him away from his friends. Then they will go without food.'

36 Then Jesus told them another picture story. 'You do not tear a piece of cloth from a new coat to mend an old one. If you do that, you will have torn the new coat. Also, the new piece of cloth will not seem the same as cloth from the old coat.

37 Bottles that people have made out of the skin of an animal teach us the same. Nobody pours new wine* into an old skin bottle. If they do, the new wine* will break the old bottle. The wine* will run out and they will lose it. And they will have destroyed the bottle. 38 Instead, people must put new wine* into a bottle that they have made out of new animal skin.

39 Also, after he has drunk old wine*, nobody wants new wine*. He says, "The old wine* is much better." '

6

What the Jews* can do on their day for rest

1 On a Jewish* day for rest, Jesus was walking through some fields where wheat* was growing. Then the men that were following him began to pick some of the wheat*. They were rubbing* the seeds with their hands. Then they were eating the wheat* that remained.

2 Some Pharisees* were walking along with them. 'You should not be doing that', they said. 'You know that it is against God's rules to work on our day for rest.'

3 'Remember what David did. He did it when he and his men were hungry', Jesus replied. 'You have certainly read about it. 4 He went into the Great House of God*. And he took the special bread that was there. It is against God's rules for anyone except the priests* to eat that bread. But he ate some of it and he also gave some to his friends.

5 The Son of Man* has authority to say what people can do on the day for rest', Jesus said.

Jesus makes a man well on their day for rest

6 On another Jewish* day for rest, Jesus went into the meeting place and he taught. A man was there. His right hand was very small and weak. The man could not use this hand. 7 Some teachers of God's rules and some Pharisees* were careful to watch Jesus. They wanted a reason to say that he was doing wrong things. If he made this man well, they would say, 'Jesus is not obeying the rules that God gave. He works on the day for rest.' 8 But Jesus knew what they were thinking. So he spoke to the man. 'Get up and stand in front of everyone.' The man got up and he stood there. 9 'Let me ask you something', Jesus then said to the people. 'What should we do on the day for rest? Do God's rules say that we should do good things? Or do they say that we should do bad things? Should we save the life of someone? Or should we destroy a life?' 10 Nobody replied. So Jesus looked round at everyone. 'Put out your hand', he said to the man. When he put it out, it became well. He could use it again.

11 Then the Pharisees* and those that taught God's rules were very angry. They began to talk to each other. 'What can we do to Jesus?' they said.

Jesus chooses the 12 men

12 One day Jesus went up a hill to pray. He remained there all
night and he was talking to God. 13 In the morning, he asked all
those that were following him to come to him. Then he chose
12 of them that he would send out with his message. These 12
men were called apostles*. These are their names:

14 Simon. Jesus called him Peter.
Andrew. He was the brother of Simon.
James,
John,
Philip,
Bartholomew,
15 Matthew,
Thomas,
James, the son of Alphaeus,
Simon the Zealot*,
16 Judas, son of James,
Judas Iscariot. He sold Jesus to those who wanted to
kill him.

Jesus tells a special message

17 After Jesus had chosen the 12 men, they all came down the
hill. He stopped and he stood on a flat place. A large crowd
of those that were following stood with him. There were also
many people from Jerusalem and from the towns of Judea
and the coast of Tyre and Sidon. 18 These people had all come
to hear Jesus teach. Those that were ill wanted him to make
them well. He was also making well those people that had bad
spirits*. 19 All the people were trying to touch him, because he
was making each person well with his great power.

Jesus teaches those that follow him

20 Jesus looked at those that were following him. He spoke this
message to them.

'Listen, you that are poor. You are children of God, so
be happy.'

²¹ 'Listen, you that are hungry now. God will feed you, so
be happy.'

²² 'People may hate* you, because you obey me, the Son of
Man*. They may say that you are very bad. They may cause
you to go away. They may do other bad things to you. When
that happens, be happy. ²³ After all, God will give you many
good things when you go to his home. So, be very happy! Jump
up and down because you are so happy. Think about those
that do bad things to you now. It was their fathers* that also
did the same bad things long ago. They did bad things to those
that spoke messages from the Holy Spirit*.

²⁴ Listen, you that are rich now. And listen, you that have a
comfortable life. Trouble will come to you.

²⁵ Listen, you that are full now. You will be hungry.

Listen, you that are laughing now. You will be sad and you
will cry.

²⁶ Trouble will happen to you, if people always say good things
about you. Your families* long ago said the same good things
about bad people. Those bad people said that they spoke
messages from the Holy Spirit*. But they did not.'

Love people that want to hurt you

²⁷ 'I say this to you who are listening carefully to me', Jesus
said. 'Love people that want to hurt you. Do good things to
people that hate* you. ²⁸ Say good things to people that say
bad things to you. Pray for people that do bad things to you.

²⁹ Someone may hit you on one side of your face. If he does,
let him hit the other side of your face too. Someone may take
away your coat. If he does, do not stop him from taking your
shirt too. ³⁰ Give to anyone that asks you for things. Someone
may take things that are yours. If he does, let him keep them.

Do not ask for them back again. ³¹Do to other people the good things that you want them to do to you.

³²Do you only love people that love you? If you do, you are not doing anything special. Do not want people to speak well about you because you love like that. After all, even bad people love those who love them. ³³Do you only do good things to people that do good things to you? If you do, you are not doing anything special. Do not want people to speak well about you for that. After all, even bad people do the same. ³⁴Do you lend things only to people that will give your things back? If you do that, you are not doing anything special. After all, even bad people lend things to other people. They believe that they will get them back again. ³⁵No! I am telling* you to love people that want to hurt you. Do good things to them. Lend things to them and do not want to get them back again. If you do this, the high God will give you a great gift. He is kind even to people that do not say "thank you". He is even kind to bad people. So you will really be his sons. ³⁶So be kind, as God your Father is kind.

³⁷Do not say to someone, "You are a bad person." If you do not, God will not say to you, "You are bad person." Do not say to people, "God should punish* you because you are bad." If you do not, they will not say that to you. Forgive* other people and God will forgive* you. ³⁸Give to other people and God will give to you. He will give to you more than you gave. He will fill your pocket until no more will go in. It will be so full that it will come out over the top. How you give to other people, God will give to you.'

³⁹Jesus also used this picture story to teach the people. 'A blind* man cannot lead another blind* man. If he does, they both will fall into a hole in the ground.

⁴⁰A student is less important than his teacher is. But when the student has learned everything, he will be like his teacher.

⁴¹Perhaps you want to tell your brother about his mistake. If you want to do that, first remember your own mistakes. ⁴²If

you do not, you are like this: You are like a person that has a piece of wood in his eye. That person then says, "Brother, you have some dirt in your eye. Let me take it out for you." Do not be like that person. You say one thing but you do something different yourselves. First, make right your own mistakes. Only then can you know how to tell another person about his mistake.'

A picture story about a tree and its fruit

43 'Good trees only make good fruit. Bad trees only make bad fruit. 44 So in this way you can know if a tree is good or bad. You can know by the fruit that it makes. You only pick good fruit from good fruit trees and bushes. Figs* do not grow on thorn* bushes. Grapes* do not grow on briers*.'

45 'People are the same. A good man brings good things out of his mind. His good thoughts are very valuable. A bad man brings bad thoughts out of his mind. He values the bad things inside his mind. So, when a person speaks, his words show something. They show whether his mind is full of good thoughts or bad thoughts.'

A picture story about men that are building a house

46 'Do not call me, "master, master", and then not obey me', said Jesus. 47 'Some people hear my message and they obey it. Let me tell you what those people are like. They are like a man who built a house. 48 This man dug down to the rocks. He put the first line of stones on the rock. After that, he built the house on top of the rock. Then a storm came and it brought a lot of water. The water hit the house but it could not move it. The water could not move the house because the man had built it very well.

49 Some other people hear my message but they do not obey it. Let me tell you about those people. They are like another man who built a house. This man did not dig down deep to the rock. Instead, he put the first line of stones on the ground and

he built on them. Then a storm came and it brought a lot of water. It hit this house and it fell down immediately. The water completely destroyed it.'

7

A Roman* officer believes that Jesus can help him

¹After Jesus had finished speaking to the people, he went to Capernaum. ²A Roman* officer there had a servant that he loved. The servant was very ill and he was dying.

³The officer heard about Jesus, so he sent some of the Jewish* leaders to speak to him. 'Please go to Jesus', he said to them. 'I would like him to make my servant well. Ask him if he would come to do that.' ⁴The Jewish* leaders then went to Jesus. 'Please would you do something for this Roman* officer', they were saying. 'Please would you go and make his servant well. ⁵This man loves the Jewish* people. He himself built a meeting place for us.'

⁶So Jesus started to go with them. When he was not very far away from the house, the officer sent some friends to talk to him. He told them that they should say. 'Sir, I do not want to be a trouble to you. I am not as important as you are. So you should not come into my house. ⁷I did not come to talk to you myself, because I am not good enough. Instead, just say a word and my servant will be well again. ⁸After all, someone also has authority over me. And so I have authority over other soldiers. I say to one soldier, "Go!" and he goes. I say to another one, "Come!" and he comes. And I say to my servant, "Do this!" and he does it.'

⁹When Jesus heard this message from the officer, he was very surprised. He turned towards the crowd that was following him. 'Listen!' he said. 'I have not found anyone like this man in all of Israel*. Nobody else believes so well in me.'

¹⁰The friends of the officer returned to his house. Then they saw that the servant was well again.

Jesus makes a dead man alive again

¹¹The next day, Jesus went to a town called Nain. Those that always followed him and a large group of other people went with him. ¹²When he had almost reached the gate of the town, lots of people were coming out. They were carrying a dead man in a box to bury him. His mother had no other sons and her husband was also dead. A large crowd from the town was with her.

¹³When the LORD Jesus saw her, he felt very sorry for her. 'Do not cry', he said. ¹⁴He went to the box and he touched it. So the people that were carrying the box stopped. 'Young man', said Jesus, 'get up, I say to you!' ¹⁵At this, the dead man sat up and he began to talk. Jesus then gave him back to his mother.

¹⁶Everyone that saw this was afraid. 'How great and powerful God is', they said. 'An important servant of God has appeared among us. God has come to save his people.'

¹⁷This news about Jesus went all through Judea. It also reached the people in the countries that were near there.

Jesus talks about John the Baptist*

¹⁸Then some men went to visit John the Baptist* in prison. Those people obeyed what he taught them. They told him about Jesus and about all that he was doing. So, John chose two of them. ¹⁹'I want you to go to the LORD Jesus for me', he said. 'Say to him, "John said that someone would come. John asks if you are that man. Are you the Messiah*? Or should we still look for someone else?" '

²⁰So the two men came to Jesus. 'John the Baptist* has sent us to you', they said. 'He wants us to ask you, "Are you the man that would come? Or should we still look for someone else to appear?" '

21 At that time, Jesus made many people well. They had many different illnesses. Some had bad spirits*. Jesus also caused many that could not see to see again. 22 Then he replied to the two men that John had sent. 'Go back to John', he said. 'Tell him what you have seen. And tell him what you have heard. People that could not see can see now. People that could not walk can walk now. Some had illnesses of the skin; they are now well. Some could not hear, but now they can. Some people were dead; they now live again. Poor people are hearing the good news. 23 If anyone continues to believe in me, he will be happy.'

24 The two men that followed John left. Then Jesus began to speak to the crowd about him. 'You went out to see John in the desert*. Think about what you went to see', he said to them. 'You certainly did not go to see a tall piece of grass. The wind blows grass about. John is not weak, as grass is. 25 If not that, think about what you went to see. You certainly did not go to see a man who was wearing expensive clothes. People like that have many beautiful things and they live in big houses. John is not like them. He lives in the desert*. 26 So think about what you went out to see. You went out to see a man that receives messages from God. Yes, and John was even more important than that. 27 A long time ago, God spoke about him. "Listen! I will send someone with a message from me. He will arrive first to prepare your way." '

28 Jesus also said to the people, 'Yes, John is a very important person. He is greater than any man that has lived before. But there are people that are not great. But God rules in them. Any one of those people is more important than John.'

29 A lot of people heard what Jesus said. 'What God says about us is right', they said. So they asked John to baptise* them. Some of these people took money on behalf of the government. 30 The Pharisees* and the people that taught God's rules did not want John to baptise* them. They did not believe the message that God was giving to them.

31 So Jesus continued to teach. 'I will talk to you about the people that are alive today. I will tell you what they are like', he said. 32 'They are like children who are sitting in the market place. They are playing. They shout out to other children, "We made happy music on a pipe* for you, but you did not dance. We sang a sad song and you did not cry." 33 You are like those children. When John the Baptist* came, he often went without food. He never drank wine*. So you said that he had a bad spirit* in him. 34 Then I, the Son of Man*, came. I both eat and drink. So you say about me, "Look at this man! He eats and drinks too much. He is a friend of those people who take money on behalf of the government. He is a friend of other bad people." That is what you say about us. 35 But God is wise* and good. Wise* people understand and they agree with him.'

A woman pours expensive oil* on Jesus

36 Then one of the Pharisees* asked Jesus to eat a meal with him. So Jesus went to his house and sat down to eat. 37 In that town was a woman that did many wrong things. She heard that Jesus was eating a meal at the house of the Pharisee*. So she took a small jar of oil* and she went there. The oil* was very expensive and it had a beautiful smell. Someone had made the small jar out of white stone. 38 When she went inside, she stood behind Jesus. She was crying and she made his feet wet with her tears*. Then she dried them with her hair and she kissed them. She then poured all the oil* out of the jar on to his feet. 39 When the Pharisee* saw this, he said to himself, 'This man cannot be someone that receives messages from God. If he were, he would know all about this woman. He would not let her touch him. He would know that she is a very bad person.'

40 'Simon', said Jesus to him, 'I want to tell you something.' 'Yes, Teacher, tell me', replied Simon. So he told him a picture story about two men.

41 'Someone had lent them money. He had lent one of them 500 silver* coins. He had lent the other one 50 coins.'

⁴²'Neither of the men had the money to pay him back. Then the man that had lent them the money forgave* them. "You do not need to pay back my money", he said to them both. Which of these two men will love that man most?' Jesus asked.

⁴³'I think', replied Simon, 'that it is the first man. It is the man that needed to pay back the most money.'

'You are right', said Jesus. ⁴⁴Then he turned towards the woman. 'You see this woman', he said to Simon. 'When I came into your house, you did not give me water for my feet. But she has washed my feet with her tears* and she has dried them with her hair. ⁴⁵You did not welcome me with a kiss', he went on to say. 'But this woman began to kiss my feet when she came in. And she has not stopped. ⁴⁶You did not put oil* on my head. But she has brought expensive oil* with a sweet smell to put on my feet.'

⁴⁷'So I tell you this. This woman has done many bad things. But I have forgiven* them. She loves me a lot, because I have forgiven* her a lot. If I only forgive* a little, a person only loves me a little.'

⁴⁸'Woman', Jesus then said, 'I forgive* you for all the bad things that you have done.'

⁴⁹The other people at the meal talked among themselves. 'Who is this man? Can he really forgive* the bad things that people have done?'

⁵⁰'You believed that I could forgive* you!' Jesus told the woman. 'You will not have troubles in your mind any longer. You can go now.'

8

The women that helped Jesus

¹After this, Jesus started to travel from one place to another. In each town or village, he spoke the good news to the people. 'God wants to rule in your lives', he was telling them. The 12

men that always followed Jesus were going with him. ²Some
women were also travelling with them. These women had been
ill, but Jesus had made them well again. One of the women was
Mary Magdalene. Jesus had sent 7 bad spirits* away from her.
³Another of the women was Joanna, the wife of Chuza. Chuza
had authority over all the people that worked in the house of
King Herod. Another of the women was Susanna. These and
other women were helping Jesus and the 12 men that he had
chosen. They were using their own money to do this.

The picture story about a farmer that planted seeds

⁴Large crowds of people were coming to Jesus from many
towns. A large number were already together when Jesus told
this story.

⁵'A farmer went out to plant seeds in his field. While he was
throwing the seeds, some fell on the path. Then people walked
on them and the birds ate them. ⁶Some seeds fell on ground
with rocks in it. They started to grow, but the young plants
had no roots*. Because there was no water in the ground, they
died. ⁷Some seeds fell among weeds. Then the weeds grew up
with the young plants. They stopped the young plants from
becoming strong, so they soon died. ⁸But some seeds fell on
good ground. Good, strong plants grew up from them. Each of
these plants made one hundred seeds.'

When Jesus finished the picture story, he said, 'You have ears.
So listen well to what I say.'

Jesus explains why he tells picture stories

⁹The men that always followed Jesus asked him about this
story. They asked him what it meant. ¹⁰'God helps you to
understand what these stories mean', he replied. 'But they
are a secret to other people. They do not understand how
God rules in the lives of his people. So, I tell picture stories to
teach them. They have their eyes wide open, but they do not
really see. They hear the words, but they do not understand.'

Jesus explains the picture story about the seeds

11 'This is what the story means', he went on to say. 'The seed is like the message of God.

12 Some seeds fell on the path. Some people hear the message from God, but they do not think about it. They are like the path. The devil* comes and he takes the message away from them. Because he takes it away, they cannot believe it. Because they do not believe it, God does not save them.

13 Some seeds fell on ground with rocks in it. People that are happy to hear the message of God are like this ground. But the message does not change their lives and their thoughts. They believe in God for a time. But when they have trouble or difficulty, they stop believing.

14 Some seeds fell among weeds. Some people hear the message and they believe for a time. They are like the ground with weeds. They start to think about the things of this world. They want to get money and things that make them happy in this life. These things push the message from God out from their lives, so they stop believing. They are like a plant that has no fruit.

15 Some seed fell on good ground. Some people that hear God's message are like this ground. They remember and they obey. They are good and honest. They continue to believe and they do many good things. They are like a plant that has lots of good fruit.'

16 'People do not light a lamp* and then cover it', Jesus went on to say. 'Nor do they put the lamp* in a jar or under a bed. Instead, they put it in a high place. Then other people that come into the room can see the light from the lamp*.'

17 'The message of God is the same. It is a secret to some people. But one day everyone will see everything that has been a secret.

18 So you should be careful how you listen. The person that has really heard a message will hear more. Some have not listened to it, so they have nothing. They think that they have a little. But they will lose even that.'

The mother and brothers of Jesus come to see him

19 Then the mother and brothers of Jesus came to see him. But they could not reach him because of the large crowd. 20 'Your mother and brothers are standing outside', someone told Jesus. 'They want to see you.'

21 'I will tell you who my mother and brothers are', replied Jesus. 'Some people hear the message of God and they obey it. Those people are my mother and brothers.'

Jesus stops a storm

22 One day Jesus got into a boat with those that always followed him. 'I want us to go over to the other side of the lake', he said. So, they started to cross the lake. 23 While they sailed, Jesus began to sleep. Then a strong wind started to blow across the lake. Water began to fill the boat and they were in danger. 24 So those in the boat with Jesus woke him. 'Master, master, we shall die!' they said.

Then Jesus got up and he spoke to the wind and to the water. 'Stop', he said. 'Be quiet.' The wind stopped immediately and the water became flat. 25 'You do not believe in me and you should believe', Jesus said then.

The event frightened them and they were very surprised. 'So who is this man?' they asked each other. 'He even has authority over the wind and the water. He just speaks and they obey him.'

Jesus makes a man well

26 Jesus and the 12 men that always followed him arrived at Gadara. In Gadara, the people called Gerasenes lived. This

place is across the lake from Galilee. 27When Jesus got off the boat, a man from the town came towards him. He had many bad spirits* and they were living inside him. He had not worn any clothes for a long time. He did not live in a house. Instead, he lived in a place where people buried dead bodies. 28When he saw Jesus, he screamed. Then he fell to the ground in front of him. 'What do you want to do with me, Jesus?' he said in a loud voice. 'You are the Son of the powerful God above. Please do not hurt me.' 29He said this because Jesus had spoken to the bad spirit*. 'Come out of this man', he had ordered*. People usually kept this man tied up. They tied his hands and feet with chains*. But when the bad spirit* took hold of him, he broke the chains*. The spirit* then caused him to go into the places where people do not live.

30'What is your name?' Jesus then asked. 'My name is Legion*', he replied. People called him this, because many bad spirits* had gone into him.

31The bad spirits* asked Jesus again and again not to send them to hell*.

32There was a large group of pigs and they were eating their food on the side of the hill. 'Let us go into the pigs', they asked Jesus. 'You can go into them', he replied. 33So the bad spirits* came out of the man and they went into the pigs. All the pigs rushed together down the high hill. They ran into the lake and all of them died in the water.

34The men that were taking care* of the pigs saw this happen. They ran away to tell other people about the pigs. They went to all the towns and villages that were near. 35So the people came out from all these places to see what had happened. When they arrived, they found the man. He was sitting at the feet of Jesus. The bad spirits* had gone out of him. He was now quiet and his mind was well again. He was also wearing clothes. When the people saw this, they were afraid. 36Some people had seen Jesus make the man well. They told the other people how he had done this. 37Then all the people from the country of the people called Gerasenes spoke to Jesus. 'Please leave us', they said. They said this because they were very afraid. So, he got back into the boat. He was ready to return to the other side of the lake. ³⁸ Then the man that had had the bad spirits* spoke. 'Please let me come with you', he said to Jesus. 'No', he replied. ³⁹ 'You must return to your home. Go. And tell everyone all that God has done for you.'

So the man went away. He went everywhere in the town. He continued to tell all the people, 'Jesus has done very good things for me.'

Jesus makes Jairus's daughter well

⁴⁰ When Jesus returned to the other side of the lake, the crowd was very happy to see him. They were all waiting for him to come back. ⁴¹ Then a man called Jairus came to see him. He was a ruler in the meeting place. He went down on his knees at the feet of Jesus. 'Please come to my house', he said. ⁴² 'I have a daughter. She is 12 years old and she is very ill. She will die very soon. She is the only child that I have.'

So, Jesus started to go to see his daughter. A crowd of people went with him and they were pushing against him. ⁴³ There was a woman in the crowd that had lost blood for 12 years. She had paid all her money to doctors and she had no money left. But nobody could stop her bleeding. ⁴⁴ She came behind Jesus in the crowd. Then she touched the edge of his clothes. Immediately she stopped bleeding. ⁴⁵ 'Who touched me?' asked Jesus.

Everyone round him said, 'It was not me. I did not touch you.' 'Master', said Peter, 'the people are in a crowd round you. Many people are touching you.'

⁴⁶ 'Someone did touch me', said Jesus. 'I felt it when power went out from me.' ⁴⁷ The woman knew that she could not hide it. So she was very afraid, when she came to Jesus. She went down on the ground in front of him. She spoke so that all the people could hear her. 'I wanted to be well', she told them,

'so I touched the edge of his clothes. As soon as I touched him, I became well.' 48'Daughter', Jesus said to her, 'you are well again, because you believed in me. Do not have troubles in your mind any longer.'

49While Jesus was still speaking to the woman, someone arrived from Jairus's house. 'Your daughter is dead', he told him. 'Do not ask the teacher to come now.'

50Jesus heard what the man said. So he spoke to Jairus. 'Do not be afraid. Just believe that I can make her well.'

51When they arrived at the house, Jesus would not let everyone go in. He only took Peter, James and John. He also let the mother and father of the girl go into the house. 52Many people there were crying. They were hitting themselves because they were very sad. 'Do not cry', Jesus told them. 'She has not died. She is only asleep.'

53They knew that she had died. So, they laughed* at him. 54But Jesus took hold of her hand. 'My child, get up', he then said to her in a loud voice. 55She became alive again and she stood up immediately. 'Give her something to eat', he said to her parents. 56They were very surprised. 'You must not tell anyone what has happened', he said to them.

9

Jesus sends out the 12 men that always followed him

1Jesus asked the 12 men that always followed him to come to him. Then he gave them power to make sick people well. He also gave them authority to send bad spirits* out of people. 2Then, he sent them out to tell other people about how God rules in the lives of his people. He told them also that they should make sick people well. 3'When you go', he said, 'take nothing for your journey. Do not take a stick, a bag or food. Do not take any money or two sets of clothes.'

⁴'Find a house where the people in it are happy to have you. Stay at that house all the time you are visiting people in that town. ⁵In some towns, the people will not be happy to see you. They have not believed the message that God sent to them. When you are leaving them, clean the dirt of that town from your feet. This shows them that they have not believed the message.'

⁶Then the 12 men that followed Jesus started out. While they were going from one village to another, they talked to all the people. They told them the good news about Jesus and they made many sick people well.

A ruler hears about Jesus

⁷Herod the ruler heard reports about all that was happening. He was confused because people were saying different things about Jesus. Some were saying, 'John the Baptist* has come back and he is alive again.' ⁸Some were saying, 'It is Elijah that has come back.' Some other people were saying, 'This is one of God's servants that died a long time ago. He is alive again and he speaks messages from the Holy Spirit*.'

⁹'My soldiers killed John', Herod said. 'They cut off his head. So, who is this man? I hear strange stories about him.' So, he was trying to meet Jesus.

Jesus feeds 5000 men and their families

¹⁰The 12 men that Jesus had sent out returned from their journeys. They told him what they had done. Then he took them away from the crowd, so that he could be alone with them. They went in the direction of a city called Bethsaida. ¹¹But the crowds found out where they were going. So they went to find Jesus. When he saw the crowds coming, he received them well. He told them how God rules in the lives of his people. Some sick people were there and he made them well.

12When it was nearly evening, the 12 men that always followed Jesus came up to him. 'This is a place without houses', they said. 'Send the crowd away now, so that they can buy food. There are some villages and farms near here. Maybe they can sleep there.'

13'You give them something to eat', said Jesus.

'But we only have 5 loaves of bread and 2 fish', they replied. 'Do you want us to go and buy food for all these people?' 14There were about 5000 men in the crowd.

'Say to them that they should sit down on the ground in groups', Jesus replied. 'There should be about 50 people in each group.'

15So they did this. When the people had sat down, 16Jesus took the 5 loaves and the 2 fish. Then he looked up towards the sky and he thanked God for the food. He broke it into pieces. And he gave it to the 12 men that always followed him. 'Give it out to all the people', he said. 17Everybody ate and they all had enough. Then they picked up all the food that remained. They filled 12 baskets with it.

Peter says who Jesus is

18Jesus was alone and he was praying. The 12 men that always followed him came up to him. 'Who do the people say that I am?' he asked them.

19'Many people say that you are John the Baptist*', they replied. 'Some people say that you are Elijah. Other people say that you are one of the servants of God from long ago. They say that the servant has become alive again.'

20'What do you think?' Jesus then asked them. 'Who do you say that I am?'

'You are the Messiah*', replied Peter. 'God sent you.'

21'Listen!' Jesus then said to them. 'You must not tell this to anyone, that I am the Messiah*.' He said this very strongly.

²² 'They will cause the Son of Man* to have a lot of pain', he went on to say. 'The leaders of the Jews* will be against him. The important priests* and teachers of God's rules will also not accept him. They will kill him, but three days later God will cause him to be alive again.'

²³ Then Jesus spoke to all the people that were there. 'Perhaps someone wants to obey me', he said to them. 'That person must say no to what he wants for himself in this life. He must live every day like a person that has only one day to live. He must obey me and he must become like me.

²⁴ After all, whoever wants to keep his own life will lose it. But whoever gives up his life for me will save it. ²⁵ Perhaps you want to get the whole world and all that is in it. You might do that but lose yourself. Then you will have nothing at all. You will have destroyed yourself in the end. ²⁶ Perhaps you are now ashamed of me and of my words. If you are, I will be ashamed of you. I will be ashamed of you when I return. When I come back again, everyone will see me. I will look* as great and beautiful as my Father God. The good angels* of God will be with me, too. They will also look* very great and beautiful.'

Jesus looks* different and he meets Moses and Elijah

²⁷ 'Listen!' said Jesus. 'Some people that are standing here will soon see how God rules. They will see this before they die. They really will.'

²⁸ About 8 days after Jesus had said these things, he went up a mountain to pray. And he took Peter, John and James with him. ²⁹ While he was praying, his face began to look* different. His clothes also became very white and shining. ³⁰ Then two men appeared and they were talking with him. They were Moses and Elijah.

³¹ Moses and Elijah looked* very great and beautiful. They talked with Jesus about how he would soon die in Jerusalem. This was how God wanted him to leave this world.

32 While this was happening, Peter was very, very tired. And those that were with him were very, very tired too. Then they really woke up and they saw Jesus. He looked* very great and beautiful. They also saw the two men that were standing near to him. 33 Then the two men began to leave. So, Peter spoke to Jesus. 'Teacher', he said, 'it is very good that we are here. We should build three huts. One hut will be for you, one hut for Moses and one hut for Elijah.' He did not really know what he was saying.

34 While Peter was speaking, a cloud appeared. And it covered them all. When the shadow covered them, they were afraid. 35 Then they heard a voice from the cloud. 'This is my Son', the voice said. 'I have chosen him. So listen to him.'

36 The voice stopped speaking. Then the three men saw that they were alone with Jesus. They did not tell anyone at this time about what they had seen.

Jesus makes a boy well

37 The next day, Jesus and the three men that were with him came down from the mountain. A large crowd met him. 38 Then a man from the crowd shouted to him. 'Teacher, please, I ask you to be kind to my son. He is my only child. 39 Sometimes a bad spirit* quickly takes hold of him and he screams. The spirit* throws his body first one way then another and foam* comes out of his mouth. When the spirit* leaves him in the end, it has always hurt him. 40 I asked those that follow you to send the bad spirit* out of him. But they could not do it.'

41 'You people today do not believe in God', Jesus said to the crowd. 'You have turned away from him. I have already been with you a long time. But you still do not believe in him. It is difficult to be patient with you.' Then he spoke to the man. 'Bring your son here.'

42 While the boy was coming, the bad spirit* threw him to the ground. It pulled the boy first one way and then the other.

'Stop!' Jesus said to it. He then made the boy well and he gave him back to his father.

43 Everybody was very surprised at what they saw. They knew that God was very powerful.

Jesus speaks again about his death

The people were still thinking about everything that Jesus was doing. Then he began to talk to those that always followed him. 44 'Be careful. And do not forget what I am telling you. People will give the Son of Man* to powerful men to kill him.' 45 But they did not understand what he had said. It was still a secret, so they could not understand his words. But they were afraid to ask him, 'What do you mean?'

Who will be the most important?

46 Then those that followed Jesus began to argue with each other. 'Which of us is the most important?' 'I am', they were each saying. 47 Jesus knew what they were thinking. So he picked up a small child. He made the child stand at one side of him. 48 'If someone accepts this child because of me', he said, 'he accepts me. And he also accepts him who sent me. After all, the person who makes himself the least important is really the greatest.'

49 'Teacher', John then said, 'we saw a man. He was speaking to people that had bad spirits* in them. "Jesus says that you must come out", he was saying. We told the man that he must not do this. We said that because he is not in our group.'

50 'Do not try to stop him', Jesus said to him. 'If someone is not against you, he is working with you.'

People in a village in Samaria do not accept Jesus

51 Time was passing and soon Jesus would go back to God. He knew this, so he began to go to Jerusalem. 52 He arrived near a village in the country of Samaria. Then he sent some people

to the village with a message. They went to ask for a place to stay for the night. ⁵³But the people in the village would not let him stay there. This was because he was going to Jerusalem.

⁵⁴Then James and John heard about what had happened. 'Jesus', they asked, 'do you want us to ask God to send fire down from the sky? Do you want us to kill these people?'

⁵⁵Jesus turned round. 'No!' he said, 'do not do that. That would be very wrong.' ⁵⁶Then they all went on to another village.

What it costs to obey Jesus

⁵⁷When they continued on their journey, a man spoke to Jesus. 'I will follow you. And I will go where you go.'

⁵⁸'Wild animals', he replied, 'have a place to sleep. Wild birds also have their own places to live. But I, the Son of Man*, have no regular place to lie down and rest.'

⁵⁹'Come with me!' Jesus then said to another man. 'First', he replied, 'let me go home and bury my father. Then I will come with you.'

⁶⁰'No!' said Jesus, 'let dead people bury their own dead people. You go. And tell other people about how God rules.'

⁶¹'Sir', said another man, 'I will come with you. But please let me first go to say goodbye to my family.'

⁶²'A man that ploughs a field must continue to look in front of him', replied Jesus. 'If he looks behind him, he cannot plough well. You are like a man that wants to look behind him. People like that cannot show other people how God really rules.'

10

Jesus sends out 72 men that always followed him

¹After this, Jesus sent out another 72 men that always followed him. He sent them on in front of him in pairs. They

went to every town and village that he would visit soon.
² 'Many people are wanting to believe God's message', he said
to them before they went. 'They are like a field with many
plants with ripe* seeds. But there are very few workers to
bring in the ripe* seeds. So, you must pray to God to send out
workers. They will go and tell his message.'

³ 'I am sending you out', Jesus went on to say. 'So go! But
listen! You will be like young sheep among wild animals. ⁴Do
not carry a purse or bag. Do not take extra shoes. When
you meet other people on the road, do not waste time in
long conversations.'

⁵ 'When you go into a house, first say, "We pray that all will
be well with you!" ⁶Someone in the house may believe what
you say. If he does, it will be well with him. But if nobody
accepts your kind words, take them back. ⁷While you are in
the town, you should stay in the same house. Accept the food
and drink that the people in the house give to you. This is for
the work that you are doing. Do not go from one house to
another to get food. ⁸The people may accept you when you go
into a town. Eat what those people give to you. ⁹Make the sick
people well in that town. Give this message to all the people
there: "We bring the news that God wants to rule in your lives
now." ¹⁰Sometimes when you go into a town, the people will
not accept you. You should then go into the streets of that
town and you should say to the people, ¹¹ "There is dirt from
your town on our feet. We will clean it off to show that you
have not accepted the message from God. Listen! God wants
to rule in your lives, but you have refused him." ¹²One day God
will judge* everyone. At that time, he really will punish* the
people from that town. Yes, he will punish* them more than
the people that lived in Sodom.'

Some towns where people did not believe

¹³ 'It will be bad for you, people of Chorazin', Jesus went on to
say. 'It will be bad for you, people of Bethsaida. I have done
great things in your cities. If I had done such great things in

Tyre and Sidon, the people there would have listened to me long ago. They would then have put on clothes made from the hair of a goat. They would also have put ash on their heads. This would show God that they were sorry. They would have stopped doing bad things and they would have started to obey him. 14 Yes, when God judges* everyone, he will punish* the people of Tyre and Sidon. But he will punish* more the people of Chorazin and Bethsaida.

15 And the people in Capernaum, they try to lift themselves up to God's place. But he will throw them down to hell*!'

16 'The person that listens to you, listens to me', Jesus told those that he was sending out. 'The person that does not accept you does not accept me. And the person that does not accept me also does not accept someone else. He does not accept him who sent me.'

The 72 men return

17 Later, the 72 men that Jesus sent out returned to him. They were very happy. 'Master', they said, 'even bad spirits* obey us. We use your name and we say, "Leave!" Then they leave.'

18 'I was watching and I saw the devil* fall', replied Jesus. 'He fell very fast, like lightning* from the sky. 19 Listen! I have given authority and power to you. You will even stand on dangerous snakes and insects and you will have authority over all the power of the devil*. Nothing will hurt you. 20 But do not be happy just because you have authority over bad spirits*. Your names are in the book where God is. That is why you should be happy.'

Jesus is very happy

21 At this moment, the Holy Spirit* made Jesus very happy. 'Father', he said, 'you rule all things above and on the earth! I thank you for this. You have taught people that do not know many things. Now they can understand this. But you have hidden all these things from other people. They think that they

understand everything. And they think that they are wise*. Yes, Father, this is how you chose it to happen.'

22 'My Father has given me all things', he then said. 'Only the Father knows who I am. Nobody else really knows that I am the Son of God*. Only I know who the Father is. Nobody else knows, except those people that I choose to tell.'

23 Then he turned. And he spoke only to those that always followed him. 'Be happy! God has helped you to see the things that you see. 24 Listen! There have been many rulers. Many men have received messages from God. Those people all wanted to see the things that you are seeing. But they did not see them. They wanted to hear what you are hearing. But they did not hear it.'

This is a picture story about a good man from Samaria

25 A man that taught God's rules then stood up. He wanted to show that Jesus really did not know the rules well. So he asked a question. 'Teacher, what must I do to live for all time?'

26 'What do God's rules say?' Jesus asked. 'What do you understand from them?'

27 'It says that we should love* the LORD our God', he replied. 'We should love* him very much, with every part of our body and of our mind. We should also love people that live near to us. We should love them as much as we love ourselves.'

28 'You have told me the right answer', said Jesus. 'If you do this, you will live for all time.'

29 But the man wanted to show that he had been right to ask a question. So he asked, 'Who are the people near to me that I must love?'

30 Jesus answered by telling a picture story. 'A man was going down the road from Jerusalem to Jericho town. On the way, some men attacked him. They took away all his clothes and they hit him with sticks. He was almost dead when they left

him. ³¹But it happened that a priest* was going down that road. He saw the man, who was lying there. But he walked past him on the other side of the road. ³²A Levite* was also going down the road. He came to the place where the man was lying. He saw him. But he also walked past on the other side of the road.'

³³ 'But a man from Samaria was also travelling along the road. And he came to the place where the man was lying. When he saw him, he felt very sorry for him. ³⁴He went across to him. He poured oil and wine* on the places where he was bleeding. Then he tied those places with clean cloths. After that, he put the man on his own animal. They arrived at a small hotel. He took him in and he was kind to him.'

³⁵'The next day, the man from Samaria took out two silver* coins from his purse. He gave the money to the man that was taking care* of the hotel. "Be kind to this man for me", he said. "I will return. This money may not be enough. I will pay you for any more that you have spent on him." '

³⁶Then Jesus asked the man that taught God's rules a question. 'Three men passed the man that was lying on the road. Which of them showed love to him?'

³⁷'It was the man that was kind to him', he answered.

Then Jesus said to him, 'Yes, you are right. So go and do the same for other people.'

Jesus visits the home of Martha and Mary

³⁸Jesus and those that always followed him continued their journey. They arrived at a certain village. There, a woman called Martha asked Jesus to come into her house. ³⁹This woman had a sister called Mary. Mary sat down near Jesus. She was listening to the things that he was teaching. ⁴⁰But Martha was thinking to herself, 'I cannot do all this work alone.' So she came to Jesus. 'Master', she said, 'my sister is not helping me with the work. She has left me to do it alone.

You cannot really believe that this is right! Say to her that she must help me!'

⁴¹'Martha, Martha', replied Jesus, 'you have troubles in your mind about very many things. ⁴²But only one thing is really important. And Mary has chosen it. Nobody will take it away from her.'

11

Jesus teaches those that always followed him how to pray

¹One day, Jesus was praying in a certain place. He finished praying. Then, one of those that always followed him came to him. 'Master', he said, 'John taught those that followed him how to pray. Please teach us as he did.'

²'When you pray', he replied, 'you should say this:

"Father, we want all people to know that you are good and important.
You will rule everyone one day.
We pray that that day will come soon.
³ Please give us the food that we need each day.
⁴ Forgive* us for all the wrong things that we have done.
After all, we also forgive* everyone that has done wrong things to us.
Do not let us agree to do wrong things." '

⁵He then told a picture story to teach them how to pray. 'Let me tell you about someone that goes to a friend at midnight. "My friend", he says, "please give me three loaves of bread. ⁶Another friend of mine is on a journey and he has arrived at my house. But I have no food to give him." ⁷But his friend answers from inside his house. "Do not cause problems for me! I have locked my door. My children and I have gone to bed. So, I cannot get up and give you any bread." ⁸I will tell you what will happen. Perhaps the friend will not give him anything

because they are good friends. But if he continues to knock, he will get up. If he continues to ask for bread, his friend will give him bread. He will give him everything that he asks for.

9 So I tell you this. Continue to ask for what you need. And you will receive it. Continue to look for what you need. And then you will find it. Continue to knock at the door and God will open it for you. 10 After all, everyone that asks for something will receive it. Everyone that looks for something will find it. God will open the door for everyone that knocks on it. 11 Some of you are fathers. You would not give your son a snake if he asks for fish! 12 If your son asks you for an egg, you would not give him an insect to hurt him. 13 You are bad. But you know how to give good things to your children. And your Father above knows much better than you do how to give good things. So he will send the Holy Spirit* to those people that ask him.'

Jesus teaches the people about the devil*

14 One day, Jesus was ordering* a bad spirit* to come out of a man. Because of the bad spirit*, the man could not speak. But after it had gone out of him, the man could speak. All the people that were watching were surprised at this. 15 But some people in the crowd were not happy with Jesus. 'Yes, this man can cause bad spirits* to come out from people', they said. 'But the devil* works with him, because the devil* rules all the bad spirits*.'

16 Some other people in the crowd did not believe in Jesus. They wanted to show that his power was not from God. 'Do something powerful', they were saying. 'If you do, we will believe. We will believe that God has sent you.'

17 But Jesus knew what those people were wanting. 'If groups of people in a country fight each other', he said to them, 'they will destroy their own country. If people in one family fight with each other, they will destroy their family. 18 The devil* is the same. The people who obey him must not fight each other. If they do, he will soon not have anybody to rule. But you say

that the devil* helps me to send bad spirits* out of people. If
this were true, the devil* would be fighting himself. He would
soon not have anybody to rule. ¹⁹You say that the devil* helps
me to cause bad spirits* to leave. But some men obey what
you teach. And they also cause bad spirits to leave. So think
about who helps them to do that. That shows that you are
wrong. ²⁰So when I cause bad spirits* to leave people, I use
the power of God. This shows that God is ruling among you.

²¹When a strong man has all his arms for war, he can take
care* of his own house. Nothing bad will happen to his things
inside the house. ²²But someone may come that is stronger
than he. Then the stronger man attacks him and beats him.
The stronger person then takes away all his arms for war.
These arms had made him feel safe. The stronger man will also
give away all the things that he had taken.'

²³'If someone is not helping me, he is against me. If a person
is not working with me to bring people together, he is causing
them to run away from me.'

²⁴'When a bad spirit* goes out of a person, it travels through
dry places. It goes to look for a new place to live. If it does
not find anywhere, it says to itself, "I will return to the house
where I lived before." ²⁵It goes back to that house. But it finds
that it is clean. Everything inside is in the right place. ²⁶So it
goes out and it brings back 7 worse spirits*. They all go into
the house and they live there. Now the man is worse than he
was at the beginning.'

²⁷While Jesus was saying this, a woman in the crowd shouted
out. 'How happy is the woman that gave birth to you! How
happy is the woman that fed you from her breasts!'

²⁸'How happy, rather', he replied, 'are the people that hear the
message from God. That is if they obey it.'

Jesus talks about Jonah

29 The crowd round Jesus was growing larger, so he began to speak to them. 'The people that are alive today are very bad. They want God to show them some powerful work. But God will not show them anything. They will only see the same powerful thing that happened to Jonah. 30 Something happened to him. It showed the people in Nineveh that God had sent him. The same thing will happen to me, the Son of Man*. I will be like Jonah to the people that are living today. Then they will know that God sent me.'

31 'Many years ago', Jesus then said, 'the queen of a country in the south travelled a long way to see King Solomon. She went to listen to the wise* ideas that he taught. Listen! There is someone here today that is greater than Solomon. But you will not listen to him. So, when God judges* all people, that queen will stand in front of him. And she will speak against the men that are alive today. After all, she travelled a long way to hear the wise* ideas of Solomon.'

32 'Jonah is the same. When he spoke to the people in Nineveh, they stopped doing bad things. And they obeyed God. Listen! There is someone here today that is greater than Jonah. But you will not obey him. God will judge* all people. Then those men that lived in Nineveh will stand in front of him. They will also speak against the people that are alive today. After all, when Jonah spoke to the people in Nineveh, they stopped doing bad things. And they obeyed God.'

Jesus talks about being full of light

33 'When someone lights a lamp*, he does not hide it. Nor does he put a pot over it. Instead, he puts it in a high place, so that people will see the light. They will see it when they come in. 34 Your eyes are like a lamp*, and your body is like a room. If a lamp* is clean, the whole room has light. But if it is dirty, the whole room is in the dark. 35 So, be sure that your eyes are not

like a dirty lamp*. If they are, you will be bad, like a dark room.
³⁶So, your eyes should be like a clean lamp*. There will be
nothing bad in you. You will be like a room that is full of light.'

³⁷While Jesus was speaking, a Pharisee* asked him to eat a
meal with him. So, he went to his house and he sat down at
the table. ³⁸Jesus did not wash his hands before he ate the
meal. This surprised the Pharisee*. ³⁹So the LORD Jesus spoke
to him. 'You Pharisees* are like someone that only cleans the
outside of a cup and plate. You only clean the part that people
can see. But inside, your mind is full of very bad thoughts. You
think about taking valuable things from other people. ⁴⁰What
fools you are! The God that made the outside of you also
made the inside. He sees everything inside you. ⁴¹So give to
poor people with good thoughts. So then God will say that
everything inside and outside of you is clean.'

⁴²'You Pharisees* give to God one tenth of the little plants
that have a nice smell. You also give him one tenth of the little
plants that cause food to taste nice. You are right to give
them. But trouble will happen to you, because you do not also
do the most important things. You do not love God*. And you
do not do what is right. You should do these. And you should
also give him a tenth of what you grow.

⁴³Trouble will happen to you Pharisees*, because you like to
have the best seats in the meeting place. And people speak to
you in the market place as they speak to an important person.
You like that too.

⁴⁴Yes, you want to seem good but you are not. So trouble will
happen to you. Sometimes, when people bury a dead body,
they do not put a mark there. Because of that, other people
walk on that ground. You are like that ground. You seem good
but, inside, you are not.'

⁴⁵Then one of those that taught God's rules spoke out.
'Teacher', he said, 'when you say these things, you are also
saying bad things about us.'

⁴⁶'Trouble will also happen to you that teach God's rules', Jesus replied. 'You give rules to people to obey. They are like things that are too heavy to carry. You put them on their backs, but you do not help them to carry them. Not even with one finger do you help them!'

⁴⁷'Yes, trouble will happen to you that teach God's rules! A long time ago, your fathers* killed the men that spoke for God. Now, you build up beautiful stones to remember the place where they buried them. ⁴⁸You know that your fathers* killed these men. You build up these stones. So you show that you agree with your fathers. You agree with what they did. ⁴⁹God is wise*. That is the reason that he said, "I will send men that I choose. I will also send other men that receive messages from me. They will speak my messages. But people will kill some of them. They will do bad things to some of them." ⁵⁰People have killed those that speak for God since the beginning of the world. But he will punish* the people alive today for all those murders. ⁵¹Abel was the first to die and Zechariah was the last. They killed him between the Great House of God* and God's special table. The priests* kill and burn animals as a gift to God on that special table. Yes, God will punish* the people who are living today for all those murders.

⁵²Trouble will happen to you that teach God's rules. You have not taught other people to understand the messages from God. They wanted to find out what is true. You yourselves have not found out. And you have also stopped the people that wanted to know. So they could not find out.'

⁵³Then Jesus left that place. The Pharisees* and those that taught God's rules started to be very much against him. They were asking him many difficult questions. ⁵⁴They were trying to cause him to say something wrong. They were waiting to take hold of him if he did.

12

Jesus tells* the people to be careful how they live

¹While all this was happening, many thousands of people were present. There were so many people that they were almost walking over each other. Jesus began to talk first to those that always followed him. 'Do not become like the Pharisees*. They want other people to think that they are good. But they are not. They are like yeast* that causes bread to grow.'

²'People do things secretly, but everybody will know about those things. And people say things secretly, but everybody will know about those things. ³You have said things in the dark of the night. But people will hear those things in the light of day. You have said things into someone's ear behind a door that you have shut. But people will shout out all those things from the tops of the houses.

⁴You are my friends, so I tell you this. Do not be afraid of those people that can kill your body. After that, they can do nothing worse to you. ⁵I tell you that you should be afraid of God. He has the power to kill and to throw people into hell*. Once more I am telling you, be afraid of him.

⁶People sell 5 small birds for 2 coins of little value. But each little bird is valuable to God. He takes care* of them all. ⁷He does the same for you. He even knows how many hairs there are on your head. So, do not be afraid of people. You are of more value to God than very many small birds.

⁸I also say this to you. Say to other people, "I obey Jesus." If you do, I, the Son of Man*, will say to the angels* of God, "That person is someone that obeys me." ⁹But another person who knows me will say, "I do not know Jesus. I do not obey him." If he does, I will say to the angels* of God, "I do not know this person. He does not obey me."

10 Somebody may speak against the Son of Man*, and God will forgive* him. But somebody may speak against the Holy Spirit*. And he may say that the Holy Spirit is bad. God will never forgive* that person.'

11 'People will take you into places for meetings. They will cause you to stand in front of rulers and other people that have authority. These men will ask you questions. But do not be afraid of them. Do not think, "I do not know how to answer them." 12 When the time comes, the Holy Spirit* will teach you. He will tell you what to say.'

Jesus tells a picture story about a rich fool

13 Someone in the crowd spoke to Jesus. 'Teacher', he said, 'I have a problem with my brother. Our father died. Tell* my brother to give me my part of what our father left us.'

14 'It is not my job to say which of you is right or wrong', he replied. 'And it is not my job to say what each of you should have.' 15 Then he spoke to all the people. 'Think well and be very careful! Do not want more than you need. The life of a person is worth more than the things that he has. Even if he is very rich, that is still true.'

16 He then told them a picture story. 'A man had some very good ground, where he planted seeds. The plants grew very well. And he had much more than he planted. 17 He thought about how much he would soon have. "I have nowhere to store all the seeds from my plants", he said to himself. 18 But then he decided what to do. "I will pull down the building", he said to himself, "where I now store my seed. Then I will build a bigger building to store it all. There I will also keep everything else that is mine. 19 Then I will say to myself:

You have plenty of things stored away. These will be enough for you for many years. Now you can live an easy life. Eat and drink. Enjoy yourself."

20 But God said to the man, "You are a fool. Tonight you will die. You will have to leave everything behind. Think about all your things that you have stored away. Think about what will happen to them. Think about who will have them." '

21 'Some people think only about having many things for themselves', Jesus went on to say. 'That picture story is for those people. But God says about them, "They have nothing of value at all." '

Do not have troubles in your mind

22 'So I tell you that you should not be always thinking about things', Jesus then said to those that always followed him. 'Do not be always thinking about the food that you need to stay alive. Nor be always thinking about the clothes that you need to wear. 23 After all, your life is more important than your food. Your body is more important than your clothes.

24 Think about the birds. They do not plant seeds in the ground, nor cut down plants to eat. They have no buildings to store food. But they do not go hungry. God gives them food. You are of much more value than the birds.

25 Your life is the same. Even if you are always thinking about your life, you cannot make it any longer. 26 No, you cannot do a small thing like that. So, do not always be thinking about the things that you need. 27 Think about how the wild flowers grow. They do not work or make clothes for themselves. But I tell you this about them. It is true that King Solomon wore very beautiful clothes. But even one wild flower is more beautiful than he was. 28 It is God that gives beautiful clothes to wild flowers and grass. And they are alive in the field for a very short time. After that, people burn them. Yes, God gives clothes to those flowers, so he will do much more for you. He will give you all that you need. You do not yet believe in him very well.'

29 'Food and drink are the same. Do not always be thinking about the food and drink that you need. 30 People that do not

know God are always thinking about these things. That is true. But your Father, God, knows that you need them. ³¹Instead, always be thinking about the things that are important to him. Let him rule you. So then he will also give you the things that you need. ³²Yes, you are only a small group of people, but do not be afraid. After all, your Father, God, has chosen you to rule with him. ³³Sell what you have and give the money to poor people. Do good things. So you will have things of great value when you live in God's home. There your things will never become old. Their value will never decrease. Nor can anyone take them from you. No insect can destroy them there. ³⁴After all, you will want to be in the same place as the things that are of value to you.'

Be ready for Jesus to return

³⁵'Always be ready for my return. Be like those that are ready to start work. They have put on their clothes so that they are ready for work. And they have lit their lamps*.

³⁶You must be like servants that are waiting for their master to arrive. When he returns home from the marriage party, he will knock on the door. His servants should be ready to open it for him immediately. ³⁷Those servants will be very happy if their master finds them awake. If he does, he will do this. He will tie his belt so that his clothes are short. He will say to them, "Sit at the table. I will come and I will give you some food." '

³⁸'The master may arrive in the middle of the night. He may even arrive just before the sun rises. But, if the master finds them awake and ready, the servants will be happy.

³⁹You must also understand this. The master of a house does not know when a robber will try to get in to his house. If he knew, he would keep awake. He would not let the robber come in and take away his things.

⁴⁰You also must be ready. The Son of Man* will come at a time when you are not thinking, "He will come now." '

Be a good servant

[41] Peter then asked Jesus. 'Master, are you only talking to us that follow you? Or is this picture story for everyone to hear?'

[42] 'Be wise*. And be a man that the master can trust*', said Jesus. 'The master will choose a man like that. He will say to him, "I want you to rule my house and the other servants. Give them food at the right time." [43] This servant will be very happy when his master comes home. His master sees that he has done everything well. So he is happy. [44] I will tell you what will happen. The master will let the servant rule over everything that he has. [45] But perhaps the servant says to himself, "My master will not come yet." So, he begins to hit the other servants. He hits both the men and the women. He eats too much. He also drinks too much and he becomes a drunk.

[46] The master of that servant will come home and he will surprise the servant. He did not think that his master would come home on that day or at that time. Then the master will punish* him a lot. He will put the servant with those people that do not obey him.

[47] A servant may know what his master wants him to do. He should get ready and obey. If he does not, his master will punish* him. He will hit him a lot. [48] But another servant perhaps did not know what his master wanted him to do. So he did the wrong things. The master will hit him because he did the wrong things. But he will not hit him as much. He did not know that those things were wrong. If masters give much to their servants, they will want a lot in return. And God wants much from the person to whom he has given much.

[49] I came to start a fire on earth. I would be happy if that fire were already burning. [50] I have a baptism* of pain to receive. I cannot rest until this has happened.'

[51] 'I did not come so that everyone will agree. Do not think that I came for that reason. No, that is not true. Instead, I came

to make people into separate groups. ⁵²From now on, because
of me, 5 people in a family will become 2 separate groups. 2
will be against the other 3. 3 of them will be against the other
2. ⁵³The father will be against his son and the son will be
against his father. The mother will be against her daughter
and the daughter will be against her mother. The mother will
be against her son's wife. And the son's wife will be against
his mother.'

⁵⁴'You see a cloud that is rising in the west', Jesus then said
to the crowd. 'Immediately you say, "It will rain." And the
rain does come. ⁵⁵Sometimes you know that the south wind
is blowing. So you say, "It will be very hot weather." And the
hot weather does come. ⁵⁶You want other people to think that
you understand many things. So, you look at the earth and
the sky. And you say what weather will come. Yes, you know
how to do that. So look at the things that are happening near
you now. They show you what will soon happen. But you do
not understand what they are showing you. And you should
know it.'

⁵⁷'Also, you should know what these things mean for you. You
should do what is right. ⁵⁸After all, something like this may
happen to you: Someone says, "You have a debt and you have
done something wrong." So he takes you to the judge*. Before
you arrive at the office of the judge*, try to agree with this
man. If you do not agree together about the matter, it may be
bad for you. He will say to the judge*, "This man has not paid
me back my money." So the judge* will say to his officer that
he should put you in prison. ⁵⁹I tell you what will happen then.
You will not leave there until you have paid back all the debt.'

13

Stop doing wrong things or die

¹At that time, some people were standing near to Jesus. They
told him what happened to some people from Galilee. They

were burning animals as a gift for God. Pilate sent some soldiers to kill them.

2 'So think about these people from Galilee', Jesus replied. 'Perhaps you think that they had done more bad things than other people from Galilee. And so that is why they had to die. 3 No, they were not worse than other people. All of you have also done many bad things. So, you must turn away from all bad things and you must turn to God. If you do not, I tell you this. You will also die as they did.

4 And you remember what happened to those 18 people in Siloam. A high building fell and it killed them. Perhaps you think that they had done more bad things than the other people in Jerusalem. 5 No, they had not. All of you have also done many bad things. So, you must turn away from all bad things and you must turn to God. If you do not, I tell you this. You will also die as they did.'

Jesus tells a picture story about a fig* tree

6 Then he told this story. 'A man had a garden where he grew fruit. He had planted a fig* tree there. But when he came to look for fruit, he could not find any.

7 "Look", he then said to his gardener, "For three years, I have come to look for fruit on this tree. But I have never found any. So cut the tree down! I do not think that it should be here. It is wasting the ground."

8 "Master", the gardener replied, "leave the tree in the ground for one more year. Let me dig round it and let me put some dirt from animals on it." '

9 ' "If I do that, next year, the fig* tree may have some fruit on it. If it does not, I will cut it down for you." '

Jesus makes a sick woman well again

10 One day, Jesus was teaching in a meeting house. It was the Jewish* day for rest.

11 There was a woman there that had a bad spirit* inside her. It had lived there for 18 years and it had made her ill. She had to bend her back all the time. She could not stand up straight. 12 Jesus saw her. 'Woman, come here', he said. 'You are better from your illness.' 13 He put his hands on her and immediately she could stand up straight. 'How great you are!' she said to God. 'How good and powerful you are!'

14 But the leader of the meeting house was angry. He was angry because Jesus had made a sick person well on their day for rest. So he spoke to the people. 'There are 6 days each week when we should work', he said to them. 'Come on any of those days and get well. But you should not come on our rest day to get well.'

15 'You are wrong', the LORD Jesus said to him. 'You say one thing and you do something different yourselves. You each take your ox* or your donkey* outside on the day for rest. You then give them water to drink.'

16 'Look at this woman', he went on to say. 'She is in the family* of Abraham. But it is like a bad spirit* from the devil* has kept her tied up for 18 years. So it is certainly right to make her free* on our day for rest.' 17 These words caused the leaders of the meeting place to feel ashamed of themselves. But all the people there were very happy. They were happy because they had seen Jesus do many good and powerful things.

Jesus tells picture stories about seeds and yeast*

18 Then he told them a story. 'I will tell you about the place where God rules. For example, 19 it is like a very small seed. A man takes it and he plants it. He puts it in his garden and it grows. It then grows into a tree. It is so big that birds can make a place to live among the branches.'

20 'Here is another example. The place where God rules is like this', he went on to say.

21 'It is like yeast*. A woman takes some and she puts it in three large bowls of flour. Then the yeast* grows and it goes through all the flour.'

This is a picture story about a narrow door

22 Jesus was continuing his journey to Jerusalem. On the way, he went through towns and villages. In each one, he taught the people. 23 One day, somebody asked him a question. 'Sir, will God only save a small number of people?'

24 'Do your best to go in by the narrow door', he said to the people. 'I tell you that many people will want to go in. But they will not be able to get in. 25 Soon the master of the house will get up and he will shut the door. And then you may still be standing outside the door. You will knock and you will say, "Master, open the door for us to come in." "I do not know where you come from", he will reply. "I do not know you." 26 "But Master", you will begin to say, "we had meals with you. You taught us in the streets of our villages."

27 "No!" he will tell you, "I do not know you. All of you have done very bad things, so go away from me."

28 Then you will cry because you are outside. You will bite on your teeth because you are in pain. You will see Abraham and Isaac and Jacob in the place where God rules. You will also see all the people that brought messages from God there. But God will shut you outside. 29 At that time, people will come from the east and from the west. They will also come from the north and from the south. They will all come to the place where God rules. There they will sit down together to eat a special meal. 30 At that time, some people that are now last will be first. Some people that are now first will be last.'

31 At this moment, some Pharisees* came to Jesus. 'Go away from here', they said to him. 'Go somewhere else because Herod wants to kill you.'

³²'Herod is a bad man', replied Jesus. 'Tell him that I am still causing bad spirits* to come out of people. I am still making sick people well again. I will continue to do all these things for a little longer. Then I will have finished my work. ³³But I need to continue my journey for a little longer. After all, only in Jerusalem do people kill those that speak messages from God.

³⁴Oh, you poor people of Jerusalem! You kill those that speak God's messages to you. And you throw stones to kill those that God has sent to you. Many times, I have wanted to bring all of you near to me. A female bird brings all her babies together and she covers them with her body. But you would not let me keep you from danger, as she keeps her babies. ³⁵So listen! The place where you live will become like a desert*. I tell you this. One day you will say, "Happy is the man that God sends here with his authority." But until you say that, you will not see me again.'

14

Jesus goes to the house of a Pharisee*

¹One Jewish* day for rest, Jesus went into the house of a leader of the Pharisees*. This man had asked him to come and to eat a meal with him. They were all watching him carefully. ²A sick man came up to him. His arms and legs had become too large, because they were full of water. ³So Jesus spoke to those that taught God's rules. He also spoke to the Pharisees*. 'If we make someone well on our day for rest, are we obeying the message of God or not?'

⁴But they would not say anything. So, he took the sick man and he made him well again. Then he let him go away. ⁵'Think', said Jesus. 'You have a son or an animal that falls into a well on a day for rest. Think about what you do. You pull the animal out of the well immediately. Do you not do that even on a rest day?'

⁶They had to agree. They could not say anything else.

7 Jesus then told a picture story to those that were sitting at the meal. He had watched how the people chose the best places to sit.

8 'When someone asks you to come to a meal', he said, 'do not sit in the best place. After all, a man that is more important than you may come later. 9 Then this might happen if you are sitting in the best seat. The man that asked you to the meal might say to you, "Give your place to this man." Then you will feel ashamed that you sat there. You will have to move to the lowest place and sit there. 10 Instead, when someone asks you to a meal, you should do this. Go and sit in the least important place. So the man that asked you will see you there. And he may say to you, "Friend, move up to a better place." Everyone who is sitting at the table will see this happen to you. So they will know that you are an important person. 11 It will be the same where God rules. Some people may put themselves in an important place. God will send them all down lower. But he will send the man that puts himself in a low place to a higher one.'

12 Jesus also spoke to the man that had asked him to the meal. 'When you give a meal at midday or in the evening, do not ask your friends to come. Do not ask your brothers or your family. And do not ask the rich people that live near you. If you do, they will later ask you to eat at their house. This will pay you for the meal that you gave to them. 13 Instead, when you give a big meal, you should ask the poor people to come. Ask people that have lost an arm or a leg. And ask people that cannot walk very well. And ask people that cannot see. 14 Do this because they cannot later ask you to eat at their houses. So you will be happy because they cannot pay you for the meal. Instead, God will pay you. One day, people that have obeyed God will become alive again. On that day, God will pay you for what you did for those poor people.'

Jesus tells a picture story about a big meal

15 The men at the table heard what Jesus said. 'One day, there will be a big meal in the place where God rules. How happy are

those people who will eat together at that big meal', one of the men said.

16 Jesus answered him by telling a story. 'One day an important man made a big meal. He asked many people to come to eat in his house. 17When the meal was ready, he sent his servant out to tell them. So, the servant went to those that his master had asked. "Come now", he said. "The meal is ready for you." 18 But each person gave a reason why he could not come to the meal. "I have bought a field", said the first man. "So I must go out and see it. Please say that I am sorry. Tell your master why I cannot come to his meal." 19 "I have bought 5 pairs of oxen*", the next man said. "So I am just going to see if they work well together. Please say that I am sorry. Tell your master why I cannot come to his meal." 20 "I have just married", said the third man. "That is why I cannot come to the meal." '

21 'The servant went back to his master. He told him what everyone had said. Then the master of the house was very angry. "Go out quickly to every street in the town", he said to his servant. "Bring the poor people here. Bring those that have lost an arm or a leg. And bring those that cannot walk well. And bring those that cannot see." 22 The servant did that. Then he came back to his master. "Sir", he said, "I asked all these people to come to your meal. But there are still some empty places at the table." 23 The master spoke to his servant again. "Go out to the roads outside the town. Look for people by the side of the road. Order* them all to come, so that my house is full. 24 But I tell you this. None of the people that I asked at the beginning will eat the meal." '

What it will be like to obey Jesus

25 Many people were travelling with Jesus on his journey. So he turned towards them. 26 'If someone wants to obey me', he said, 'he must live like this: He must love his own father and mother less than he loves me. He must love his wife and his children less than he loves me. He must love his brothers and sisters less than he loves me. He must even love himself less than he

loves me. If he does not do that, he cannot obey me. ²⁷He must live like a person that will die very soon. Yes, if he is not ready to die for me, he cannot obey me. So think about what it will be like to obey me.'

²⁸'Here is an example. One of you wants to build a tall building. Before he starts to build, he will sit down. He will decide how much it will cost. He needs to know if he has enough money to finish the building. Think about it. ²⁹If he does not do this, he may not have enough money. He can put the lowest stones in the ground, but he cannot finish the building. If he then has to stop, other people will laugh at* him. They will say to each other, ³⁰"That man is a fool. He started to build, but he could not finish." '

³¹Then Jesus gave them another example. 'A king wants to fight a war against another king. But before he goes to fight, he sits down. He thinks to himself. "Can I win this war? My army is large, but the other king has twice as many soldiers in his army. ³²No, I cannot do it. I know I cannot beat the other king." So, while the stronger king is far away, he sends a man with a message. He tells the king that he does not want to fight. He wants to know what he can do to become a friend of the stronger king. ³³It is like that for all of you', Jesus then said. 'You must leave everything behind you. Only then, can you come and obey me.

³⁴So remember this. Salt is good. But if you mix the salt with something else, it is no longer any good. You cannot cause it to taste like salt again. ³⁵You would not put it on your field. It cannot make the ground good. You would throw it away. You have ears. So, listen well to what I am saying.'

15

¹One day, all the people that had done many bad things were coming round Jesus. Some were people that took money on behalf of the government. They all wanted to hear what Jesus was saying. ²The Pharisees* and those that taught God's rules

did not like this. They thought that it was wrong for him to be
friendly to people like that. 'This man is friendly to people that
have done bad things', they said. 'He even eats with them in
their homes.'

Jesus tells a picture story about a
sheep that a man has lost

3 So Jesus told them this story.

4 'Think about a man that has a hundred sheep', he said. 'He
may lose one of them. Think about what he does. He leaves
all the other sheep in the country where nobody lives. Then
he goes. And he looks for the sheep that he has lost. He
looks until he finds it. 5 When he finds the sheep, he is very
happy. He lifts it up and he puts it across his shoulders. 6 Then
he carries it back home. He speaks to all his friends and to
the people that live near him. He asks them to come to his
house. "I have found the sheep that I lost", he says. "So come
here and we can all be happy together." 7 The same happens
when one person turns away from doing wrong things. This
makes those that live above with God very happy. They will be
happier about him, than about the many people that already
obey God.'

Jesus tells a picture story about a
coin that a woman has lost

8 'Now think about a woman that has ten valuable coins. She
may lose one of them. Think about what she does. She lights
a lamp* and she sweeps inside her house. She looks carefully
until she finds the coin. 9 Then she speaks to all her friends and
to those that live near to her. She asks them to come to her
house. "I have found the coin that I lost", she says. "So come
here and we can all be happy together."

10 The same happens when a person turns back to God. This
makes the angels* of God very happy.'

Jesus tells a picture story about two sons

[11] Jesus then told another story. 'There was a man that had two sons. [12] The younger son went to his father. "Father, please give me now my part of your things", he said. So, the father gave both sons their part of his things. [13] After a few days, the younger son sold what his father had given to him. Then he left home. He took with him the money and everything that he had. He went on a long journey to a country far away. He wasted all his money there and he did many bad things. [14] Then after he had spent everything, something bad happened in that country. There was almost no food anywhere. So, the young man had nothing to eat. [15] He went to a man from that country and he asked for work. The man sent him into his fields to watch his pigs. [16] Nobody gave him anything to eat. So he even wanted to eat the food that the pigs were eating.

[17] Then the son began to think about what he had done. "My father has many servants", he said to himself, "and they have plenty of food to eat. They even have extra food. But I shall die here because I do not have any food. [18] So I will go to my father. 'I have done bad things against God', I will tell him. 'And I have done them against you. [19] So I am not good enough for you to call me your son any longer. Instead, please accept me as one of your servants.' "

[20] So he stood up and he returned to his father. But he was still a long way from the house when his father saw him. He felt very sorry for his son and he ran towards him. Then he put his arms round him and he kissed him. [21] "Father", the son said, "I have done bad things against God and against you. So I am not good enough for you to call me your son." [22] But the father shouted to his servants. "Hurry!" he said. "Fetch the most beautiful coat that we have. Put it on him and put a ring on one of his fingers. Put shoes on his feet. [23] Fetch the young cow that we keep ready to eat on a special day. It is already fat. Kill it and prepare it. We shall eat a big meal and we shall be happy together. [24] I thought that this son of mine was dead.

But now he has returned to me alive. I thought that he had left me for all time. But now he has come home." Then they began to be happy together.

25 While these things were happening, the older son was working in the field. On his way back to the house, he heard music. He heard people who were dancing. 26 So he spoke to one of the servants. "What is happening?" he asked him. 27 "Your brother has returned", the servant replied. "Your father has killed the young fat cow for him. He did this because your brother is alive and well." 28 When he heard this, he was very angry. He would not go into the house, so his father came out. "Please come in", he said. 29 "Listen", replied the older son, "I have worked for you for many years. I have always obeyed you. But you never even killed a young goat for me. If you had done that, I could have been happy with my friends. We could have had a meal together. 30 But now this other son of yours has returned. He has wasted all the money that you gave to him. He has spent it on women of the streets. But you have killed the young fat cow just for him." 31 "My son", said his father, "you are always with me. All that I have is yours. 32 We thought that your brother was dead. But now he has returned to us alive. We thought that he had left us for all time. But now he has come home. So we must be happy together." '

16

Jesus tells a picture story about a man that thought wisely*

1 Jesus then told another story to those that followed him. 'A rich man had a servant who worked for him. The servant took care* of the money that the man had. Then some people came to tell the rich man about his servant. They said that he was wasting his master's things. 2 So the master sent someone to fetch his servant. "I am hearing bad stories about you", he said. "So write down everything that you have done with my

money and my things. After you have done this, you will stop working for me.”

3 “I must think about what I can do”, the servant said to himself. “My master will not let me work for him any longer. I am not strong enough to dig. And I would be ashamed to ask other people for money. 4 I must stop working for my master. I know what I can do then. If I do it, people will accept me into their homes.”

5 Many people had a debt that they had not paid back to the master. So, the servant asked those people to come to him. “How big is your debt to my master?” he asked the first man. 6 “I have to give him 100 barrels* of oil*”, he replied. “Here is the paper with your debt written down on it”, said the servant. “Take the paper. Sit down and write quickly on the paper - 50 barrels*.” ’

7 ‘ “And how big is your debt to my master?” he asked the next man. “I have to give him 100 baskets of wheat*”, he replied. “Here is the paper with your debt written down on it. Take the paper and write on it - 80 baskets.” ’

8 ‘The servant was not honest. But his master spoke well about what he had done. What he had done would help him later. People that do not obey God think carefully. They know how to do well with people like themselves. People that obey God often think less carefully.

9 I tell you this. People may get money in wrong ways. But you should use it to be good to those who need help. You will die, one day. Then those people will be happy to see you in that place where people live for all time.

10 If you can trust* a person with a very small thing, you can also trust* him with bigger things. And if you cannot trust* a person with a very small thing, you cannot trust* him with big things. 11 So if people cannot trust* you with money in this world, nobody will trust* you with really valuable things. 12 And

if people cannot trust* you with other people's things, nobody will give you things for yourself.

13 A slave cannot work for two masters. If he does, he will only like one of them. He will work well for one master and he will think bad things about the other one. God and money are like masters. You cannot work for both of them.'

14 The Pharisees* heard all this. They loved money, so they laughed* at him. 'You are wrong', they said to Jesus. 15 'You like it when people look at you', he replied. 'You want them to think that you are good people. But God sees inside you. He knows what you are thinking. People think that it is important for other people to think well of them. But God thinks that this is wrong.'

16 'Moses wrote down the rules that God gave to him. Other men wrote down messages that the Holy Spirit* gave to them. Those books were the only authority until John the Baptist* began to speak. From the time when John started to tell them about it, people have also heard the good news. The good news is about how God rules. Since then, everyone is really trying to get into where God rules.

17 But this does not mean that anyone can destroy God's rules. One day, God will destroy the earth and the sky. But everything that God's men have written in the book of rules must happen. 18 Sometimes, a man sends away his wife, and then he marries another woman. If he does this, he is very bad. And sometimes, a husband sends away his wife and she marries another man. This other man is also doing something wrong.'

Jesus tells a story about a rich man and a poor man

19 'At one time, there was a rich man that also had expensive clothes. Some of the clothes were purple*. And some of them were soft and white. This man had large meals every day. 20 There was also a poor man called Lazarus. He had sores* all over his skin. He lay at the gate of the rich man. 21 He was very

hungry. He even wanted to eat the bits of food that the rich man threw away. And even the dogs came and they put their tongues* on the sores* on his body. 22 The poor man then died and angels* carried him away. They put him at the side of Abraham. The rich man also died and his family buried him. 23 He went to a bad place called Hades. He was in a lot of pain there. He saw Abraham. He was far away from him. He also saw Lazarus at the side of Abraham. 24 So he shouted out, "Father Abraham, please be kind to me. Please send Lazarus to me. I am in great pain because I am in a fire. Let him put the end of his finger into some water. Let him use the water to make my mouth cool." 25 "My child", replied Abraham, "remember the time when you were alive on earth. Remember what happened then. You had lots of good things and Lazarus had lots of bad things. Now I am taking care* of Lazarus, and you are in pain. 26 But that is not everything. Between you and us, there is a hole. It is wide and long and deep. There is a reason why this hole is there. Nobody can cross from here to where you are. And nobody can cross from where you are to come here." 27 "If that is true, Father Abraham", he said, "please send Lazarus to my family. 28 I have 5 brothers that are still alive. He can tell* them not to do the same things as I did. So they will not also come here when they die. They will not be in great pain, as I am."

29 "They have the books that Moses wrote", said Abraham. "They have all the messages that other men wrote. The men that heard from God wrote them. Your family should listen to them." '

30 ' "No, Father Abraham", he said, "they will not listen to the messages that Moses and the other servants of God wrote. But if someone goes to them from among the dead people, they will listen. So then they will turn away from doing wrong things. And they will turn back to God."

31 "You say that they do not believe. They do not believe what Moses and the other servants of God said. So also they will not believe someone that comes back from among the dead people." '

17

¹'Some people will try to cause other people to do wrong things. You can be sure about that', Jesus said to those that always followed him. 'But God will punish* every person that tries to do that. ²So he must stop doing it. If not, he should ask someone to hang a big stone round his neck. Then people should throw him into the sea with the stone. So he will not cause one of these little people to do wrong things.'

³'Be careful how you think. If your brother does something wrong, talk to him about it. Your brother may say, "I am sorry for what I did. I will not do it again." If he says that, you must forgive* him. ⁴Your brother may do a bad thing to you many times in a day. He may turn to you many times and say, "I am sorry for what I did. I will not do it again." If he does that, you must forgive* him.'

⁵'Help us', said the 12 men that Jesus had chosen, 'to believe more and more in you.'

⁶'The amount that you believe in me is not even as big as a small seed', the LORD replied. 'If it was as big as that, you could say to this tree, "Pull yourself out of the ground and plant yourself in the sea." And the tree would obey you.

⁷Think about this. You have a servant that is ploughing. Or you have a servant that is taking care* of your sheep. When he comes in from his work, you would not say to him, "Sit down and eat." ⁸No, you would not say that. You would say to him, "Prepare the evening meal for me. Get yourself ready and bring the food to me. I will eat and drink first. You can eat when I have finished." ⁹Servants should do what their masters order* them to do. Their masters do not thank them when they do that. ¹⁰It is the same with you. The Master tells you what you should do. And you do it. "We are not special* servants", each of you should say to himself. "We have only done what we should do." '

The 10 men that had leprosy*

¹¹On his journey to Jerusalem, Jesus was travelling along the border between Samaria and Galilee. ¹²When he was going into a village, 10 men came towards him. These men had an illness of the skin. They stopped some way away from Jesus ¹³and they shouted, 'Jesus, Master, please be kind to us.'

¹⁴Jesus saw them standing there. 'Go and show yourselves to the priests*', he answered. While they were going there, they became well again. ¹⁵Then one of these 10 men saw that Jesus had made him well. He turned back and he started to shout out, 'God is very good. He has made me well.' ¹⁶He went down on his knees in front of Jesus. 'Thank you, Master', he said. This man was from Samaria.

¹⁷'I made 10 men well again', Jesus said. 'There should be another 9 men! ¹⁸Only this one man came back to thank God, and he is from Samaria. There should be other men that came from Israel*.'

¹⁹Then he spoke to the man. 'Stand up again and go on your way. You believed in me, so now you are really well.'

Jesus talks about the time when God will rule

²⁰Then some Pharisees* asked Jesus a question. 'When will God begin to rule here?'

'You will not see anything different when God begins to rule here', Jesus replied. 'People will not see it happen. ²¹Nobody will say, "Look everyone! God is ruling here", or "Look! God is ruling over there." No, it is not like that. God is already ruling in the lives of his people.

²²The days are coming when you will really want to see me return', he said to those that always followed him. 'But you will not see me. ²³At that time, people will say to you, "There he is!" or "Here he is!" But do not go out with them to look. ²⁴After all, when lightning* shines, it makes the whole of the

sky light. It will be like that when I return. Everyone will see me. 25 Before this happens, the people alive now will say, "We do not want Jesus to be our king. Kill him!" And I will feel much pain.'

26 'Remember the report about the time when Noah was alive. Remember what happened then. My return will happen quickly too. 27 While Noah was making his boat, people were eating food. And they were drinking. Men and women were marrying. They continued to do all this until the day when Noah went into his boat. Then it rained for a long time and the deep water killed all the people.'

28 'The same things happened when Lot was alive. People in the city called Sodom were eating. And they were drinking. They were buying and selling things. They were planting seeds and they were building houses. 29 But then, Lot went away from Sodom. On that same day, God caused it to rain fire and burning stones from the sky. This killed all the people in Sodom. 30 The same things will happen on the day when I show myself.

31 On that day, this is what people must do. If they are outside their house, they must not go back inside to get their things. In the same way*, people that are working in the fields must not return to their house. They must not go back for the things that were in the house. No, they must just run away from Jerusalem. 32 Remember what happened to Lot's wife.'

33 'Whoever wants to save his life will lose it. But if he loses his life for me, he will save it. 34 I tell you this. At that time, two men will be sleeping in bed at night. The angels* will take one of them and they will leave the other one behind. 35-36 Two women will be working together in the same place. The angels* will take one of them and they will leave the other one behind.'

37 'Where will this happen?' those that followed Jesus asked him. 'If a dead body is lying somewhere, vultures* will come together', he said to them.

18

Jesus talks about how to pray

¹Then Jesus told those that always followed him a picture story. It taught them that they must not get tired. But they must go on praying. ²'In a certain city', he said, 'there was a judge*. He did not think that either God or people were important.'

³'A woman lived in that same city. Her husband had died. She continued to come to the judge* with a problem. "Please keep me safe from the person that is against me", she was saying. ⁴For a time, the judge* would not do anything for her. Later, he thought about himself. "I do not think that either God or people are important. ⁵But this woman causes me trouble. If I do not do anything for her, she will continue to come to me again and again. She will make me very tired. So, I will help her. I will say that she is right." '

⁶'This judge* was not a good man', Jesus said. 'But you should think about what he said to himself. He will only help because the woman causes him trouble. ⁷But God always helps those that he has chosen to be his children. When they continue to ask him for help, he will answer them immediately. He will not wait. ⁸I tell you this. He will say that they are right. He will help them quickly. I shall return to earth. But I will not find many people that still believe in me then.'

Jesus tells a story about two men that were praying

⁹Jesus also told another picture story to teach people. Some people thought that they were very good. They also thought that they were better than other men.

¹⁰'One day, two men went into the Great House of God* to pray. One man was a Pharisee*. The other man received money on behalf of the government. ¹¹The Pharisee* stood by himself. And he prayed where other people could see him. "Thank you, God,

that I am different from all these other people. They rob. They are bad. They have sex with women that they have not married. Thank you also that I am different from this man. He receives money on behalf of the government. ¹²I stop eating on two days of each week. I give to you one tenth of all that I receive."

¹³But the other man stood very far away. He would not even look up to the sky.

He was hitting his body with his hands to show how sorry he was. "Please, God, be kind to me", he was saying. "I have done many bad things." '

¹⁴'Let me tell you about these men when they went home', said Jesus. 'The man that received money on behalf of the government was now right with God. But the Pharisee* had not made anything right with God. Some people say that they are good. God will say to them, "Go away from me. You are not good." Other people know that they are not good. God will say to them, "Come up here. I have made you good." '

Jesus is with little children

¹⁵People were even bringing little children to Jesus. They were doing this so that he could touch the children. But those that always followed Jesus saw this. So they said to them, 'Stop bringing all these children here.'

¹⁶Then Jesus shouted out to them. 'Let the children come to me. Do not try to stop them. God rules in the lives of people that are like these children. ¹⁷Let me tell you something important. You must receive God as a child does. If you do not, God will never rule in your life.'

Jesus meets a rich ruler

¹⁸A Jewish* ruler came to Jesus. 'Good teacher', he asked, 'what should I do so that I can live for all time?'

¹⁹'Why do you say that I am good?' said Jesus. 'Nobody is good, except God. ²⁰You know the rules of God. Do not have

sex with anyone that is not your wife. Do not kill anyone. Do not rob anyone. Only say true things about people. Love your father and your mother.'

²¹'I have obeyed all these rules since I was 12 years old', he replied.

²²Jesus heard what he said. 'You still need to do one thing', he said. 'You must sell everything that you have. Give the money to the poor people. So, then you will have many valuable things in the place above, where God lives. Then come back and obey me.'

²³When the ruler heard this, he became very sad. This was because he was very rich.

²⁴Jesus saw that the ruler had become sad. 'It is very difficult for rich people to ask God to rule in their lives', he said. ²⁵'After all, it is difficult for a big animal to pass through the hole in a needle*. But it is even more difficult for a rich man to ask God to rule in his life.'

²⁶'So who will God save?' asked the people that were listening to Jesus.

²⁷'God can do things that no man can do', he replied.

²⁸'Listen!' said Peter, 'we have left everything to obey you.'

²⁹'Let me tell you something important', replied Jesus. 'Some people leave their home to obey God and to let him rule in their lives. They may leave their wife, their brothers, their parents and their children. ³⁰These people will receive, in this life, very much more than they left. And after they die, they will have something else. They will have a life that does not have an end.'

³¹Jesus took the 12 men that he had chosen away from the other people. 'Listen!' he said. 'We are going to Jerusalem. When we are there, many bad things will happen to me. A long time ago the servants of God wrote down messages from the Holy Spirit*. Everything that he told them about the Son

of Man* will now happen to me. 32 This is what he said. The Jews* will give me to those that are not Jews*. They will laugh at* me. They will do bad things to me. They will spit* on me. 33 They will hit me with a whip* and then they will kill me. But after three days, I will become alive again.'

34 The 12 men that Jesus had chosen did not understand any of these things. Something hid these things from them. So they did not know what Jesus was talking about.

Jesus makes a man well that cannot see

35 When Jesus was getting near to Jericho, a man was sitting by the side of the road. This man could not see and he was asking people to give him money. 36 Then he heard a large crowd of people who were passing by him. So, he asked the people near him what was happening.

37 'Jesus from Nazareth is passing by', they replied.

38 The man began to shout out. 'Jesus, Son of David*, please be kind to me.' 39 The people that were walking in the front of the crowd tried to stop him. 'Be quiet!' they were saying to him.

But he started to shout even louder. 'Son of David*, please be kind to me!'

40 Then Jesus stood still. 'Bring that man to me', he said. Then when the man came near, Jesus spoke to him.

41 'What do you want me to do for you?'

'Sir', he replied, 'please cause me to see again.'

42 'See again', said Jesus. 'You are well now because you believed in me.'

43 Immediately the man could see again. He started to follow Jesus. He was saying, 'God, you are very great and powerful.'

Many people saw what had happened. 'God, how great and important you are', they also said.

19

Zacchaeus meets Jesus

¹Jesus went into Jericho and he was walking through the city. ²There was an important man there called Zacchaeus. He took money on behalf of the government and he had become very rich. ³He was trying to see who Jesus was. There was a big crowd there and he was a small man. So he could not see him. ⁴So he ran on in front of the crowd and he climbed up a tree. He could see Jesus more easily from the tree, because he would walk along that way. ⁵When Jesus came to the tree, he looked up. 'Zacchaeus, come down quickly', he said. 'Today I must stay in your home.'

⁶So Zacchaeus came down quickly and took him into his home. He was very happy about this. ⁷The people saw what had happened. And they were not happy. 'Jesus has gone to stay in the home of a man that does bad things', they were saying.

⁸Zacchaeus then stood up in front of everyone and he spoke to the Master. 'Listen, Master', he said. 'I will give half of all that I have to poor people. I have taken too much money from some people. I will give them 4 times as much as I took from them wrongly.'

⁹⁻¹⁰'Today', said Jesus to him, 'God's salvation* has come to this home. After all, I came to look for people that God has lost. And I have come to save them. And Zacchaeus is also part of the family* of Abraham.'

Jesus tells a picture story about 10 servants

¹¹ While the people were still listening, he told them a story. He did this because he was getting near to Jerusalem. He knew that the people had wrong thoughts. They had wrong thoughts about what would happen there. They were thinking that God would begin to rule his people immediately after that.

¹²'An important man left his home and he travelled a long way to another country', he told them. 'There he would receive authority to rule his own country. After that, he would return as king. ¹³Before he left, he asked 10 of his servants to come to him. He gave each of them 10 pounds of silver*. "Use this money to get more money for me while I am away", he said.'

¹⁴'The people who were living in his country did not like the man. So, they sent a group of people after him with a message. That message was: "We do not want this man to rule over us."

¹⁵When the king returned, he asked those 10 servants to come to him. He wanted to know how much more money they had made from his money. They should have bought things with it and then they should have sold those things again for more money.

¹⁶The first servant came. "Master", he said, "your money has made 10 more pounds."

¹⁷The master was happy. "You have done well. You are a good servant that I can trust*. You have used a small amount of money well. So you will rule over 10 cities."

¹⁸The second servant came. "Master, your money has made 5 more pounds."

¹⁹"You will rule over 5 cities", the Master said to him.

²⁰Then another servant came. "Master", he said, "here is your money. I put it away in a piece of cloth. ²¹I did this because I was afraid of you. After all, you tell people what they should do all the time. You take things that you did not work for. You do not put seeds in the ground, but you take the plants from the fields."

²²"You are a bad servant", the Master replied. "I will use your own words to show you that you have done the wrong thing. You said that you know about me. That I tell people what they should do all the time. That I take things that I did not work for. That I do not put seeds in the ground, but I take plants

from the fields. ²³You should have put my money into the bank. When I came home, I might have had my money back again with extra." ²⁴Some other servants were standing near to their master. "Take the money from this servant", he said to them. "Give it to the servant that has 10 pounds."

²⁵ "But, Master", they replied, "that servant has 10 pounds already."

²⁶ "Let me tell you this", the Master said. "Some people have something. To them I give more. Other people have nothing. From them I take away even the small thing that they have. ²⁷Now I must punish* these other people that did not want me to rule over them. Bring them here and kill them in front of me." '

Jesus goes into Jerusalem

²⁸ When Jesus had said all this, he went on in front of them. He was going up to Jerusalem. ²⁹And he was getting near to two villages called Bethphage and Bethany. They were at the hill called the Mount of Olives*. So, he sent two of those that always followed him into one of the villages.

³⁰ 'Go into the village that is in front of you. When you go in, you will find a young donkey*. Someone has tied it up there. Nobody has ridden on it before. Remove the tie and bring the donkey here to me. ³¹Someone may ask, "Why are you taking the donkey*?" If they do, tell them: "The Master needs to use it." '

³²The two men that Jesus sent went into the village. They found everything there that Jesus had told them about. ³³While they were taking the young donkey*, some men spoke to them. It was their donkey*. They asked, 'Why are you taking the young donkey*?' ³⁴'The Master needs to use it', they replied. ³⁵They brought it to Jesus, and they put their coats on top of it. Then they helped Jesus to get on to it. ³⁶While he was riding along, the people were putting their coats down on the road.

37 Jesus got near to the lowest part of the hill called the Mount of Olives*. The whole crowd of those that followed him became very happy. 'God, how great and powerful you are', they were shouting out. 'You are very powerful. Thank you for all the great things that we have seen. 38 Happy is the King that comes with the authority of God. We want all to be well in the place above where God lives. We pray that it will be. He is beautiful. He has all power and authority.'

39 Some of the Pharisees* in the crowd spoke to Jesus. 'Teacher', they said, 'stop those people that are following you from saying these things.'

40 'Let me tell you this', replied Jesus. 'If these people were quiet, the stones of the city would shout out instead!'

41 When Jesus got near to the city, he looked at it in front of him. He cried because he felt very sorry for the people in it. 42 'You need to know what you should do, to live without trouble', he said. 'You need to be well with God. But now, something is hiding these things from you. 43 As a result, bad days will come to you. Your enemies will build a wall round you. They will shut you in completely, and they will not let you leave. 44 You did not understand that God had come to save you. So your enemies will kill you and they will destroy your city. They will break down your walls and they will not leave one stone in the right place.'

Jesus teaches in the Great House of God*

45 Jesus went into the Great House of God*. Some people were selling things there. He began to cause them to leave. 46 'This is what God has said in his book', Jesus said. 'God has said, "My house will be a place where people come to pray." But you have made it into a place where people rob each other.'

47 Jesus was teaching every day in the Great House of God*. The leaders of the priests* and those that taught God's rules wanted to kill him. The leaders of the people also wanted to kill him. 48 But all the people were listening to him. They

wanted to hear all that he was saying. So, the leaders did not know how to kill him.

20

Jesus talks about his authority

¹One day, Jesus was teaching in the Great House of God*. He was telling people the good news about how God rules. Then the leaders of the priests* and the teachers of God's rules came to him. With them were some other Jewish* leaders. ²They all came to speak to him. 'Tell us what authority you have to do these things', they said. 'Who gave you this authority?'

³'I also will ask you something', he answered them. 'Tell me this. ⁴John had authority to baptise* people. Did this authority come from God or did someone else give it to him?'

⁵The Jewish* leaders talked to each other about his question. 'We could say that God gave John authority. But if we say that, Jesus will say to us, "So why did you not believe him?" ⁶Or we could say that someone else gave him that authority. Then all the people would throw stones at us to kill us. After all, they are sure that John received messages from the Holy Spirit*.' ⁷So they answered, 'We do not know who gave John authority to baptise*.'

⁸'So, I will not tell you who gave me authority to do these things', Jesus replied.

Jesus tells a picture story about farmers

⁹ Then Jesus began to tell this story to the people in the Great House of God*.

'A man planted a field with vine* plants. He let some farmers take care* of the plants. Then he went away to another country and he stayed there for a long time.

¹⁰ When it was time to pick the fruit, the man sent a servant to the farmers. The servant said to them, "Please give me part of the fruit for my master."

But the farmers hit him with sticks and they sent him away with nothing.

¹¹ The master then sent another servant to the field. They also hit him with sticks and they did other bad things to him. They also sent him away with nothing. ¹² The master sent a third servant to the field. The farmers hurt him badly too and they threw him out of the field.

¹³ Then the master of the field said to himself, "I must think about what I should do. I know what I will do. I will send my son that I love very much. Perhaps they will be kind to him." ¹⁴ But the farmers saw him coming. "This is the son of our master", they said to each other. "When our master dies, he will have the field. We should kill him and then the field will be ours."

¹⁵ So they threw him out of the field and they killed him.'

'This is what the master will do to the farmers', said Jesus. ¹⁶ 'He will come to those farmers. He will kill them and he will give the field to other farmers.'

'That must not happen!' replied the people when they heard this. ¹⁷ Jesus then looked at the people. 'You say that this must not happen. But this is what is in God's book.

> "The builders refused to use one special stone.
>   But that stone is now the one that makes the corner of the wall strong.

¹⁸ When a person falls on to that stone, it will break their body into pieces. But when that stone falls on top of someone, it will destroy him completely." '

The leaders ask Jesus a question

¹⁹The teachers of God's rules and the priests* wanted to take hold of Jesus immediately. They knew that Jesus was talking against them in the story. But they did not do it, because they were afraid of the people.

²⁰So this is what they did to catch Jesus. They gave money to people to ask him a difficult question. These people seemed to be good, but they were not honest. Instead, they wanted to hear Jesus say something wrong. Then they would take him to the ruler of the city for him to punish* Jesus. ²¹This is what these people asked: 'Teacher, everything that you say is right. And everything that you teach is right. We know that. You do not say something different to an important person to make him happy. Instead, you teach everyone the same message. And you say what God really wants them to do. ²²Should we pay money to the Roman* leaders who rule us? Do God's rules let us do this or not?'

²³Jesus knew that the men wanted him to say the wrong thing. He knew that they only seemed to be good people. ²⁴'Show me a coin', he said to them. 'Whose picture and name are on it?'

²⁵'They are the picture and the name of the Roman* ruler', they replied.

'So give to the Roman* ruler the things that are his', said Jesus. 'And give to God the things that are his.'

²⁶So the Jewish* leaders could not cause Jesus to say wrong things about the Roman* ruler. They were very surprised at his answer to their question. This caused them to stop speaking.

The Sadducees* ask Jesus a question

²⁷Then some of the Sadducees* came to see Jesus. These men did not believe that any dead people will become alive again.

28 They asked him a question. 'Teacher', they said, 'Moses wrote this rule for us to obey. A man may die. If his wife has no children, the brother of her husband must marry her. We should call their children the children of the man that died. 29 But once there were 7 men that were brothers. One of the brothers married. Then he died but they had no children. 30 Another brother then married this woman, but he also died. 31 Then the third brother married the woman. The same thing happened to all 7 brothers. None of them had any children before they died. 32 After this, the woman also died. 33 People say this about those that have died. They say that one day they will live again. So, when that happens, whose wife will she be? After all, she had been wife to all 7 of them.'

34 'Men and women that are alive on earth get married', said Jesus to them. 35 'But dead people that live again do not marry. God has chosen some people to live again with him. He says that they are good. They do not marry 36 and they cannot die any more. This is because they live as the angels* live. They are children of God. He has made them alive again.

37 It is true that dead people live again. Moses showed us this in the report about the burning bush. He told us that our God said this: "I am the God of Abraham, the God of Isaac and the God of Jacob."

38 But God is not a God of dead people. He is God of living people. Abraham, Isaac and Jacob are alive to him. Really, he sees all people as alive.'

39 Some of the teachers of God's rules agreed. 'Teacher', they said, 'that was a very good answer.' 40 They were afraid to ask him any more questions.

The Messiah* is someone that David calls Master

41 Jesus said to them, 'Why do people say this, "The Messiah* will be someone from the family* of David"? 42 After all, David himself said this in the book called Psalms*:

"Our God said to my Master:
Sit at the place of importance, at my right side.
43 Remain there until I put your enemies under your feet.
You will rest your feet on them."

44 So David calls him Master. So how can he also be from the family* of David?'

Be careful not to do the same as those that teach the rules

45 All the people were listening. Jesus then spoke to those that always followed him.

46 'Be careful not to do the same as the teachers of God's rules. They like to wear long clothes to show how important they are. They like people to speak to them in front of many people, as they would speak to an important person. They like to have the best seats at meetings. They like to sit in the most important places at special meals. 47 They cause women whose husbands have died to supply them with money. They use this for themselves. They pray in front of many people for a long time. This causes people to think that they are good. Because they do these things, God will punish* these people a lot. It will be worse for them than for people that have not done these things.

21

Jesus talks about people who give things to God

1 Then Jesus looked at what was happening in the Great House of God*. There was a box for money there. Many rich people were putting their gifts of money into it.

2 Then he saw a woman. Her husband had died. She was very poor. She put two very small coins of little value into the box. 3 'Let me tell you this', said Jesus. 'This poor woman has put more money into the box than everyone else. 4 The rich people put in money that they do not need. They have plenty more.

This woman has less money than she needs. She needs money to buy bread to eat. But she put all of that money into the box.'

Jesus talks about things that will happen

5 Some of those that followed Jesus were talking about the Great House of God*. They spoke about the many beautiful and valuable stones in the walls. They pointed out the many beautiful gifts to God that people had put on it. 6 'You can see all these beautiful things just now', Jesus said. 'But a day is coming when enemies will destroy it all. They will throw down every stone. Not one will remain on top of another.'

7 'Teacher', they asked, 'so when will this happen? What will we see just before this happens?'

8 'Be careful', he replied. 'Do not believe things that are not true. After all, many people will come and they will say, "I am Jesus." They will say that the right time for God is soon. Do not follow those people.

9 And when you hear about wars, do not be afraid. Also, do not be afraid when people are fighting against their governments. These things must happen first. But the end will not happen immediately.'

10 'Yes', he was saying, 'people from one country will fight people from another country. And kings will send their people to fight other kings and their people. 11 The ground will move so much that people will be afraid. In many different places, plants for food will not grow; so, many people will go hungry. Illnesses will go from one person to another; so, many people will die. Many things will also happen in the sky that will frighten people. 12 But before all those things happen, these things will happen: People that hate* me will take hold of you. They will do bad things to you because you are obeying me. They will take you to their meeting places. They will bring you in front of kings and rulers. And they will ask them to put you in prison or to kill you. 13 This will be the moment to tell them the Good News about me. 14 So prepare your minds. Do not

think about how to answer the questions of kings and rulers. ¹⁵After all, I will give you the right words to speak so that nobody can argue with you. They will just be quiet. ¹⁶Even your parents and other people in your family will bring you in front of kings and rulers. They will kill some of you. ¹⁷Everybody will hate* you, because you are obeying me. ¹⁸But your life will be safe with me. You will not lose even one hair from your head. ¹⁹Yes, you will really live, if you never stop obeying me.

²⁰One day you will see Jerusalem with armies all round it. Then you will know that enemies will soon destroy Jerusalem. ²¹People in Judea must then run to the hills and hide. People that are inside the city must leave it. People that are outside the city must not go back into it. ²²This is when God will punish* Israel's* people. Then all the things will happen that his servants wrote about. ²³That time will be a very bad time for women that have a baby inside them! It will be very bad for those women that have little babies! Yes, very bad things will happen to all the people of this country. God will be very angry with them. ²⁴At that time, enemies will kill many people with sharp knives. They will take some people and they will cause them to leave their country. They will live in many other countries and they will not be free* to return to this country. People that are not Jews* will destroy Jerusalem. They will rule here until it is time for them to stop.'

²⁵'You will see strange things happen to the sun and moon and stars. On earth, the things that happen will make people in many countries very afraid. The sea will make a lot of noise and there will be big storms at sea. ²⁶This will cause trouble. And it will frighten people because they do not understand these things. The powerful things in the sky will move from their usual places. Then people will be afraid about what will happen next in the world. They will be so afraid that they will become very, very weak. ²⁷It is then that they will see the Son of Man*. I will come in a cloud with a lot of power. I will look* very important and very beautiful. ²⁸When these things begin to happen, stand up. And look up. God will soon save you.'

29 Jesus then explained to them what this time would be like. 'Think about the fig* tree or any other tree. 30 You see new leaves on the tree. Then you know that summer will come soon. Nobody needs to tell you that. 31 It will be the same when you see all these things happening. You will then know that God will soon begin to rule.

32 Let me tell you this. Some of the people alive will not die until all this has happened. 33 The sky and the earth will go away. But my message will remain true. What I have said will happen.

34 But be careful. And watch how you live. Do not eat or drink too much. Do not waste your time like that. Do not waste time by having troubles in your mind about your life. If you do, that day will surprise you. It will come when you are not looking. 35 And it will surprise everyone who lives on earth. 36 So watch all the time! Continue to pray for power to get out of all these things! So then you will stand in front of me. And you will not be afraid of me.' 37 Jesus was teaching every day in the Great House of God*. Each night he went out of the city and he stayed on the Mount* of Olives*. 38 He returned to the Great House of God* each morning. All the people were going there early to hear him.

22

Judas agrees to catch Jesus

1 The day was coming soon when the Jews* would eat a special meal of bread without yeast*. This time is called Passover*.

2 The leaders of the priests* and the teachers of God's rules wanted to kill Jesus. They were thinking about how they could do this. It was difficult because they were afraid of the people. They wanted to kill him secretly.

3 Then the devil* began to live inside Judas Iscariot. He was one of the 12 men that Jesus had chosen. 4 Judas went away and he talked to the leaders of the priests*. The police that

worked at the Great House of God* were also there. They
talked about how Judas could give Jesus to them secretly.
⁵They were very happy and they promised to give him money
for this. ⁶So Judas said that he would do it. He then began to
watch for the right moment to catch Jesus. He wanted to do it
when the crowd was not round Jesus.

Jesus eats his last meal with those that he had chosen

⁷The day came for the meal of bread without yeast*. The
people had to kill the young sheep for the Passover* meal on
this day. ⁸So Jesus sent Peter and John. 'Go and prepare the
Passover* meal', he said. 'Then we can all come and eat it.'

⁹'Where would you like us to prepare the meal?' they
asked him.

¹⁰'Listen', he replied, 'When you start to go into the city, a
man will meet you. He will be carrying a jar of water. Follow
him until he goes into a house. ¹¹You must then say to the
master of that house, "Our Teacher sends this message to
you:'Where is the room for visitors? I will eat the Passover*
meal there with those that always follow me.' "

¹²The man will show you a large room upstairs. It will have all
that you need in it. Prepare the Passover* meal there for us all.'

¹³So Peter and John went into the city. They found everything
that Jesus had told them about. And they prepared the
Passover* meal.

¹⁴When it was time to eat it, Jesus arrived. He sat down. The
men that he had chosen sat down with him. ¹⁵'I have wanted
very much to eat this Passover* meal with you', Jesus said
to them. 'It has to happen before I die. ¹⁶Yes, I will not eat
another Passover* meal after this one. I will not eat it again
until God begins to rule.'

¹⁷Then he took a cup and he thanked God for the wine*. 'Take
this cup', he said to them. 'Each of you drink some wine*. ¹⁸Let

me tell you this. From now on, I will not drink wine* until God begins to rule.'

19 Then he took a loaf of bread and he thanked God for it. He broke the bread into small bits and he gave it to each of them. 'This is my body. I am offering it up to God for each of you. When you do this from now on, remember me.'

20 Jesus did the same after the meal. He took a cup of wine* and he gave it to them. 'This is about the new promise. It is between God and his people. I will let people kill me and pour out my blood. Then this promise can start to happen.'

21 'But look! The hand of the person that will give me to the rulers is on the table with me. 22 I shall die, as God wants me to. That is true. But it will be very bad for the man that causes it to happen.'

23 'Who is the man that would do this thing?' they asked each other.

Jesus tells who is most important

24 Then they began to argue among themselves. They were arguing about which of them was the most important. 25 'Kings of countries have great authority over their people', Jesus said to them. 'Kings want people to say good things about them. And kings want people to say that they are their friends. 26 You must be different. The most important person among you must become the same as the least important person. The person that is master must become the same as the servant. 27 After all, which person is the most important? Is it the person that sits at the table? Or is it the servant that puts out the meal? Yes, it is the person that sits at the table. But I am here to be your servant.

28 You have never left me. You have been by my side when I had difficult times. 29 And now, I say that you will rule with me. My Father has said that I will rule with him. So, I also say to you that you will rule with me. 30 You will be at my table

where I rule. You will eat and drink with me. You will sit on rulers' chairs. You will judge* the people of the 12 families* of Israel*.'

Jesus tells Peter what will happen

31 'Simon, Simon, be careful to listen to me! The devil* has asked to have you all. He wants to cause all of you to stop obeying me. He will shake* you as a farmer shakes* seeds.'

32 'But I have prayed for you, Simon, that you will continue to believe in me. And you, when you have turned back to me, you must help your brothers* to be strong again.'

33 'Master', said Simon, 'I am even ready to go to prison with you. I am ready to die with you!'

34 'Let me tell you this, Peter', Jesus replied. 'Three times tonight, you will say that you do not know me. You will say it before the cockerel* makes a noise in the morning.'

35 Jesus then asked the men that he had chosen a question. 'When I sent you out without a purse, a bag or shoes, did you need anything?' 'No', they replied, 'nothing.'

36 'Now it is different', he said. 'If you have a purse or bag, take it with you. If you do not have a long sharp knife, sell your coat. Use the money to buy a knife. 37Let me tell you why. In the book of God, people wrote down everything that will happen to me. It says, "People will include me with other bad men." And this must happen to me soon.'

38 'Master', they said, 'Look, we have two long sharp knives here.'

'It is enough', he replied.

Jesus prays on the hill called the Mount of Olives*

39 Jesus left the city. And he went to the hill called the Mount of Olives*. This is what he usually did. Those that always followed him went with him.

40 He arrived at the place where he wanted to go. Then
he said to them. 'Ask God to keep you from wanting to do
wrong things.'

41 He went away from them about as far as you can throw
a stone. He bent his knees to the ground and he prayed.
42 'Father', he said, 'if you want, you can take away this time of
pain from me. But do not let me do what I want. I want to do
what you want.'

43 An angel* then came to him from God. The angel* made
him stronger. 44 Jesus began to have troubles in his mind. He
prayed again even more strongly. The sweat* on his head
became like large amounts of blood that fell to the ground.

45 He then stopped praying and he stood up again. He returned
to the 11 men. And he found that they were sleeping. They
were very tired because they were so sad. 46 'You should not be
sleeping', he said. 'Get up and pray! Ask God to keep you from
wanting to do wrong things.'

The soldiers catch Jesus

47 While Jesus was still speaking, a crowd of people and
soldiers came towards him. Judas led the crowd. He was one of
the 12 men that Jesus had chosen. He came near to Jesus to
kiss him. 48 'Surely you will not kiss me, Judas', said Jesus, 'to
show the soldiers which person to catch!'

49 Then those that followed Jesus saw what was happening.
'Should we use our long sharp knives, Master?' they asked him.

50 One of them hit the servant of the leader of the priests*. He
cut off his right ear. 51 'Enough!' said Jesus, 'Stop doing this!'
He then touched the man and made his ear well again.

52 Then Jesus spoke to the people that had come to catch him.
They were the leaders of the priests*, and the leaders of the
police in the Great House of God*. Other important Jewish*
rulers were also there.

'You seem to have come out here with sharp knives and heavy sticks. You seem to have come to catch me as you would catch a dangerous robber. ⁵³I was with you every day in the Great House of God*. You did not try to get hold of me then. Yes, this really is the time and the place for you to work. Now it is dark, and the devil* rules in the dark.'

Peter says that he does not know Jesus

⁵⁴Then they took hold of Jesus. They took him away and they brought him to the house of the leader of the priests*. Peter was following, but he did not get near them. ⁵⁵People lit a fire outside the house and they sat round it. Peter went and he sat among them. ⁵⁶A servant girl then saw Peter in the light from the fire. She looked carefully at him. 'This man was also one that followed Jesus', she said.

⁵⁷'Woman', Peter replied, 'I do not know him.'

⁵⁸After a short time, a man looked at him. 'You also are in their group', he said.

'Man', Peter replied, 'I am not one of them.'

⁵⁹After about an hour, someone else spoke. 'I am sure that this man was also with Jesus. He also is from Galilee.'

⁶⁰'Man', said Peter, 'I do not know what you are talking about.'

While Peter was still speaking, a cockerel* made a noise. ⁶¹Then the Master turned round and he looked at Peter. Peter remembered what the Master had said to him: 'Three times you will say tonight that you do not know me. You will say it three times before the cockerel* makes a noise in the morning.'

⁶²Peter went away and he cried a lot.

The soldiers laugh at* Jesus and they hit him

⁶³The men that were holding Jesus were laughing* at him. They were hitting him.

⁶⁴They tied a cloth round his head so that he could not see.
'You say that you get messages from God!' they said. 'Tell us,
who is hitting you now?' ⁶⁵And they were saying many other
bad things to him.

The leaders of the Jews* ask Jesus questions

⁶⁶When it was day, the leaders of the Jews* met together. The
leaders of the priests* were at the meeting. The teachers of
God's rules were also there. Then other men brought Jesus
into the meeting. ⁶⁷'Are you the Messiah*?' they asked. 'If you
are, tell us.'

'If I do tell you', Jesus replied, 'you will not believe me.
⁶⁸I could ask you, "Who do you think that I am?" But you will
not answer me, if I do that. ⁶⁹But from now on, I will be sitting
in the most important place. I will be sitting at the right side
of God. He is all powerful.'

⁷⁰'So, are you the Son of God*?' they all said.

'You say that I am. And you are correct', he replied.

⁷¹'We do not need anyone else to tell us what this man says.
We ourselves have heard what he has said about himself', they
said.

23

Pilate asks Jesus questions

¹All the people at the meeting stood up, and they took Jesus to
stand in front of Pilate.

²Then they all started to tell him that Jesus had done bad
things. 'We found this man when he was telling our people
wrong things', they said. 'He said that we must not give money
to the Roman* government. He also said that he himself is the
Messiah*, a king.'

³'Are you the king of the Jews*?' Pilate asked Jesus.

'The words are yours', he replied. 'But you are correct.'

⁴Pilate then spoke to the leaders of the priests* and to all that were there. 'I cannot find anything that this man has done wrong.'

⁵But they continued to speak strongly to him. 'He makes the people angry and ready to fight. He has taught these things everywhere in Judea. He started in Galilee and now he has come to Jerusalem.'

⁶Pilate heard them say 'Galilee'. So, he asked if Jesus came from Galilee. ⁷'Yes', they replied, 'he is from the country that Herod rules.' Herod was in Jerusalem at that time. So, Pilate sent Jesus to stand in front of him.

Herod asks Jesus questions

⁸Herod was very happy to see Jesus. He had heard about him and he had wanted to meet him for a long time. He was hoping that he would see Jesus do some powerful work. ⁹He asked him many questions, but Jesus did not answer any of them. ¹⁰The rulers of the Jews* stood there all the time. They were shouting out that Jesus had done many bad things. ¹¹Then Herod and his soldiers started to laugh at* Jesus. They were saying things to make him feel bad. They put a beautiful coat on him. It was one that a ruler wears. Then they sent him back to Pilate. ¹²Herod and Pilate became friends on that same day. Until then, they had not liked each other.

Pilate and the leaders of the Jews* argue about Jesus

¹³Pilate then said that all the leaders of the priests* and leaders of the Jews* must come back to him. ¹⁴'You brought this man in front of me', he said to them. 'You said that he was causing the people to be against their rulers. Listen! I have asked him some questions in front of you. But I did not find that he has done anything wrong. ¹⁵Herod also did not find that he had done anything wrong. After all, he has sent him back to me. So, you can see that this man has not done

anything bad. There is no reason for me to say, "Kill him." ¹⁶So I will order* a soldier to whip* him. Then I will let him go home.'

¹⁷(Pilate had to let one person come out of the prison at Passover* time.)

¹⁸So the crowd shouted together, 'Take this man away and kill him. We want Barabbas to come out of prison.'

¹⁹Barabbas had told the Jews* that they should fight against the Roman* rulers. He had also killed somebody in the fight. So, the rulers had put him in prison. ²⁰Pilate still wanted to let Jesus go. So, he again spoke to the crowd. ²¹But they started to shout, 'Kill him on a cross*, kill him on a cross.'

²²Pilate asked them the same question for the third time. 'Why do you want me to kill him on a cross*? What wrong things has he done? You want me to say that he should die. I have not found anything wrong that would cause me to say that. So, I will order* my soldiers to whip* him. Then I will let him go.'

²³But they continued to shout at him. 'Kill him on a cross*. Kill him on a cross.' They shouted very much. So, they got what they wanted. ²⁴Pilate said, 'Fix him on a cross*, as they want.' ²⁵They had asked Pilate to let Barabbas out of the prison. He was the man that had caused Jews* to be against the Roman* rulers. He had also killed somebody while he was fighting the rulers. He was the man that Pilate let go free*. As for Jesus, Pilate ordered* his soldiers to take him away. And he ordered* them to do what the crowd wanted.

²⁶So they started to take Jesus to the place where they would kill him. On the way, they took hold of a man called Simon. This man was from the town called Cyrene. He was coming in from outside the city. The soldiers took the cross* that Jesus was carrying on his shoulders. They said to Simon, 'Carry this for Jesus.' So, Simon carried the cross* and he walked behind Jesus.

Jesus tells what will happen to Jerusalem

27A very large crowd of people were following Jesus. There were many women among them. They were crying with loud voices. They were hitting their own bodies because they were very sad. 28So Jesus turned round and he spoke to them. 'You women that live in Jerusalem, do not cry for me. Cry for yourselves and for your children. 29Listen! Days will come when people will say, "Happy are those women that could not have babies. Happy are those women that never had babies to feed." 30Then people will begin to say, "It would be better if we were dead." They will ask the mountains to fall on top of them. They will ask the hills to cover them up.

31I am like a living tree, but men are doing this to me. Much worse things will happen! Those events will be like a fire that burns dry wood!'

The soldiers fix Jesus to a cross*

32The soldiers led two other men out of the prison. These men had done some bad things. The soldiers would kill them when they killed Jesus. 33They brought them to the place that is called 'The Skull*'. There they fixed Jesus to a cross*. They also fixed the two bad men to crosses. One of these men was on the right side of Jesus. The other was on the left side of Jesus.

34'Father', Jesus was saying, 'they do not know what they are doing. So please forgive* them.'

The soldiers then picked up the clothes that he had worn. Each soldier would have a part. So, they played a game among themselves, to know who won each piece. 35The people stood there. They were watching, but the rulers of the people were laughing* at Jesus. 'He saved other people, they say. He should save his own life! So then we will know that he is the Messiah*. We will know that God has chosen him.'

³⁶The soldiers also laughed* at him. They came up to him and they offered him cheap alcohol to drink. ³⁷'If you are the King of the Jews*', they said, 'save your own life.'

³⁸There was also a notice at the top of the cross*. 'This is the King of the Jews*', it said.

³⁹One of the men on a cross* at the side of Jesus started to speak badly to him.'If you are the Messiah*', he shouted, 'save your own life and our lives too.'

⁴⁰But the other bad man told him that he should be quiet. 'You should be more afraid of God. After all, all three of us will die. ⁴¹Both of us have done very bad things. So, it is right that we die. But this man has not done anything wrong.' ⁴²Then the man spoke to Jesus. 'Remember me, Jesus', he said, 'when you become king.'

⁴³'I promise you', Jesus replied, 'today you will be with me in Paradise*.'

Jesus dies

⁴⁴It was now about midday, but the sun stopped shining. So, the whole country was in the dark for three hours. ⁴⁵Then the curtain in the special room inside the Great House of God* tore into two parts. ⁴⁶And Jesus shouted loudly, 'Father, I give my spirit* to you.' After he shouted this, he died.

⁴⁷There was a captain there. He was watching the soldiers while they were doing their job. He saw what had happened. 'How great and powerful God is', he said. 'I am sure that this man had not done anything wrong.'

⁴⁸A very big crowd had come together to watch the men die. They saw what had happened. Then they began to go home. They were very sad, so they were hitting their own bodies with their hands. ⁴⁹The friends of Jesus were standing a long way away. The women that had followed him from Galilee were also there. All these people also saw what happened to him.

Joseph buries Jesus

⁵⁰A man called Joseph was also there. He was one of a special group of important Jewish* leaders. He was a good man that wanted to do right things.

⁵¹Joseph had not agreed with them that Jesus should die. He was from the Jewish* town called Arimathea. He was waiting for God to begin to rule his people.

⁵²So he went to see Pilate. He asked to have the dead body of Jesus. Pilate agreed to this. ⁵³Joseph then went to the place where Jesus died. He took the dead body down from the cross*. He covered it in a long piece of good cloth. He put the body into a large hole in the rock. He had caused someone dig this hole in the rock. It was a place to bury a dead body. It was the first time that anyone had used it.

⁵⁴This all happened on the day when people prepared meals for the Jewish* day for rest. It was nearly time for the day for rest to begin.

Jesus becomes alive again

⁵⁵So the women that had come with Jesus from Galilee followed Joseph. They saw the place where the hole in the rock was. They also saw Joseph put Jesus' body into the empty hole. ⁵⁶Then they returned to the house where they were staying in Jerusalem. There they prepared seeds with a strong smell and expensive oil* that had a beautiful smell. Then they stopped work because their day for rest was starting. They were obeying the rules in the book of God.

24

¹Very early on Sunday morning, they went to the place where Joseph had buried Jesus. They took with them the oil* and seeds that they had prepared. ²They arrived there. And they found that someone had rolled the stone away from in front of the hole. ³Then they went inside the hole in the rock, but

they did not find the body of the LORD Jesus there. 4They did not understand this at all. But, while they were thinking about it, two men in bright clothes appeared. 5So the women became very afraid and they bent down towards the ground.

'You should not be looking here for someone that is alive', they said to the women. 'This is a place to bury dead people. 6Jesus is not here. He has become alive again. Remember what he said to you. He said it while he was still in Galilee. 7He said, "It is necessary that someone should give me to bad men. They will kill me on a cross*. Three days later I will become alive again." '

8Then the women remembered what Jesus had said. 9They left the empty hole. They went to the 11 men that he had chosen. They then told them what had happened. They also told all the other people that had followed him. 10It was Mary Magdalene and Joanna that told the news about Jesus. Mary, the mother of James, and other women were with them. They also told the news to the 11 men. 11But they did not believe what the women said. They thought that it was just a silly story.

12But Peter got up and he ran to the hole in the rock. He bent down and he looked inside. He saw only the cloth that they had put round Jesus' body. There was nothing else. So he went home again. He was thinking about what might have happened.

Jesus shows himself to two people that always followed Jesus

13Later on that same day, two of those that had followed Jesus were going to a village. The village was called Emmaus. This village was about 7 miles from Jerusalem. 14They were talking to each other about all the things that had happened. 15While they were talking about everything, Jesus himself came near to them. He started to walk along with them. 16They saw him, but for some reason they did not recognise him. 17'What are you talking about while you walk along the road?' he asked them.

They stood still and they seemed sad. ¹⁸ Then one of them called Cleopas answered him. 'Many things have happened in Jerusalem in the last few days', he said. 'Are you the only visitor here that does not know about it?'

¹⁹ 'What things have happened?' he asked.

'The things that happened to Jesus that was from Nazareth. The Holy Spirit* gave him messages to speak. He did many very great things and he spoke powerful messages. God showed that his message was true. All the people believed him. ²⁰ Then the leaders of the priests* and our rulers caught him. They gave him to the Roman* ruler. They told the ruler that Jesus had done wrong things. They said that he should die. So, they killed him by fixing him to a cross*. ²¹ But we had hoped that God would use him to save Israel*.

Yes, there are other things too. Today is the third day since he died. ²² After all this, some women in our group surprised us today. Early this morning, they were at the place where someone had buried him. ²³ They did not find his body there. And they returned to us with a report. "Some angels* appeared to us", they said. "They have told us that Jesus is alive." ²⁴ So some people from our group went to the place where someone had buried him. They found everything the same as the women had said. But they did not see Jesus.'

²⁵ Jesus then spoke to them. 'Oh, how silly you are! You do not understand much. You are so slow to believe everything that God spoke by his servants. ²⁶ You should have known that the Messiah* had to die. Only then would he start to show how great and powerful he really is.' ²⁷ He then began to explain what Moses had taught. Then he talked about the other men that had received messages from the Holy Spirit*. He explained to them everything that the other men had written about him.

²⁸ They came near to the village that they were going to. It seemed that Jesus would continue his journey. ²⁹ But they

stopped him from going on. 'Please stay in our home with us', they said. 'It is getting late, and it will soon be night.'

So, Jesus went into their house to stay with them. ³⁰He sat down to eat with them. Then he took the bread and he thanked God for it. He broke it up and then he gave it to them. ³¹Then, their eyes became clear and they recognised him. Then immediately they could no longer see him. ³²They spoke to each other. 'It was like a fire that was burning in us. We felt it while we were walking along the road. We also felt it when he was talking to us about God's book.'

³³They immediately got up and they returned to Jerusalem. There they found the 11 men that Jesus had chosen. Other people were together with them. ³⁴All the people gave them the news. 'It is true! The Master is alive again. He has appeared to Simon!'

³⁵Then the two that had seen Jesus spoke to the whole group. They told them what had happened to them on the road. They also told how they recognised Jesus. They recognised him when he broke the bread.

Jesus appears to the group

³⁶While they were still speaking, Jesus himself stood among them. 'Do not have troubles in your mind', he said to them.

³⁷But the whole group was very surprised and afraid. They thought that they were seeing a spirit*. ³⁸'You should not be so afraid', he said to them. 'You seem to be not sure in your minds about what you can see. ³⁹But look at my hands and my feet. It is I, myself. Touch me. So you will know that I am not a spirit*. A spirit* does not have a body with skin and bones as I do. You can see that I have.'

⁴⁰When he had said this, he showed them his hands and his feet. ⁴¹This was such good news that they could not believe it. They were very happy.

'Do you have anything that I could eat?' he asked. ⁴²So they gave him a piece of fish that they had cooked. ⁴³And while they were watching, he took it. And he ate it.

⁴⁴'I told you about these things while I was still with you', he then said. 'Moses wrote about me in his book of rules. Other servants of God received messages about me. They then wrote in books what they heard. The book called Psalms* also tells about me. Everything that they wrote had to happen. And it has become true.'

⁴⁵Then he helped them to understand the messages in God's book. ⁴⁶'This is what it says. The Messiah* had to die. Then, after three days, he had to become alive again. ⁴⁷Now you must start to tell everyone the good news about me. Begin in Jerusalem and go to the people in every country of the world. Tell them that they should turn away from wrong things. Tell them that they should turn to God. When they do this, God will forgive* them. He will forgive* all the bad things that they have done. ⁴⁸You must tell people about everything that you have seen. And tell people about everything that you have heard. ⁴⁹Now listen! I will send down to you the gift that God my Father has promised you. So, you must stay in the city until this happens. Then the power of God will cover you.'

Jesus goes up to where God lives above

⁵⁰Then he led the group out of the city. They all went to a place near Bethany. He held up his hands over them all. He asked God to be good and kind to them. ⁵¹While he was praying for them, he went up away from them. God lifted him up to his home above. ⁵²They all bent down on their knees. 'How great and powerful you are', they all said to Jesus. 'How great is your power. You are very beautiful and important.' Then they returned to Jerusalem and they were all very happy. ⁵³They spent all their time in the Great House of God*. They were thanking God. And they were telling him how good he is.

WORD LIST

AD after the date when Jesus was born.

angel a servant from God that brings his messages.

apostles 12 men that Jesus chose to tell people about him.

baptise/baptism Christians baptise a person that turns away from doing wrong things. He then turns to God. God promises to forgive* the person that now wants to obey him. John baptised people. Some people think that he poured water over them. Other people think that they went right under the water.

Baptist a man who baptises* people.

barrel round thing in which you can keep oil or water.

BC before Jesus was born.

blind person that cannot see.

brier a kind of bush; it has many long sharp things called thorns.

brothers men or boys whose mother is also your mother; it can mean other people that obey Jesus; or it can mean other people who are in the family* of God.

care (take care of) be careful with.

cart thing with wheels* that people use to carry things.

chains many metal rings that join to make something like a rope*. People use it to stop a thing or person leaving.

circumcise to cut off the skin from the end of the sex part of a man or boy.

clean (here) when something is right to use because God is happy about it.

cockerel male of a bird called a hen.

cross a piece of wood that someone has fastened across another piece. People put Jesus on a cross to kill him.

desert a very dry place with very little water. People do not usually live there.

devil ruler of all the bad spirits*, often called Satan.

donkey an animal like a small horse.

evil very bad. There is nothing good in it.

family family included father, mother and children; it might also include grandfathers and those who had been born before them. The 12 families of Israel* included everyone who belonged to Israel*.

fathers people years ago that your parents came from.

fever if you have a fever, you are ill and very hot.

fig a fruit that is good to eat.

fishermen men that catch fish.

foam water with lots of air in it, on the top of the water.

forgive, forgiven to choose not to remember bad things against someone; God chooses not to remember the wrong things that someone has done.

free nobody has tied you up; you are not in prison.

grapes a fruit that people eat; or they make it into a drink that has alcohol in it.

Great House of God a building in Jerusalem where people met to worship* God.

hate not to like at all; to want to hurt someone.

hell place of pain. The devil* and all that refuse to obey God will go there.

holy like God; different and better than all other things; all good with nothing bad in it.

Holy One Messiah*, Jesus.

Holy Spirit one person of the three persons who are God. We cannot see him but he is there.

incense something that makes a sweet smell when it is burning: people burnt it in the Great House of God*.

Israel all the people born from Abraham, Isaac and Jacob, and their children. God chose Israel to be his special people. The word can also mean the land that God gave to these people.

Jew a person who is born from Abraham, Isaac and Jacob and their children.

Jewish a word that describes a Jew* or anything that is a Jew's*. judge a person with authority to say if another person is right or wrong.

judge to say what is right or wrong, good or bad.

lamp something that contains burning oil. It gives light.

laugh at laugh against someone to cause him to feel bad.

legion a group of Roman* soldiers. There were 6000 soldiers in a legion.

leprosy illness of the skin and bones. The person with this illness could not live with other people, but lived outside the town.

Levite a man from the family* of Levi. Levi was one of the sons of Jacob. We can read about this family* in Exodus and Leviticus, and in 1 Chronicles 23:28-32. Levites worked in the Great House of God*, but they were not priests*.

lightning light that you see in the sky during a storm.

liquid like water.

look how one can see a person or a thing; how a person or thing seems to be.

Lord a name for God or for Jesus.

love God obey God; let him rule in your life.

Messiah the man that God had promised to send; he would save his people.

Mount small mountain.

needle a thin sharp piece of metal. It has a small hole at one end.

net thin rope* that you tie together; you use it to catch fish.

oil not car oil, but from a fruit. People use oil to cook or for medicine; or they burn it to give light. People use special oil for a nice smell.

Old Testament first part of God's book, which the writers wrote before Jesus was born.

olive a tree with small fruits (or the fruits themselves) that people used to make oil. They burned the oil to give them light. They used it in other ways too.

order to say what another person must do.

ox/oxen large animal like a cow. Paradise people who believe in Jesus go to Paradise. They go there when they die.

Passover an important holiday for the Jews*. Each year they remember the day when God saved them. He saved them from being slaves in Egypt. Each family eat a special meal together during Passover*. All the Jews* tried to get to Jerusalem for this special holiday.

Pharisees a group of Jews*. Many of them thought that they were obeying all God's rules. But they were also obeying many rules that men had made. Those Pharisees did not like the things that Jesus taught. They did not like him because he did not obey all their rules.

pipe you blow into it to make music.

priest a man that gave gifts and burned animals as a sacrifice* to God for the Jews*; a man that God chose to do these things for him.

proverb something that people say about life.

psalm, Psalms songs about God that tell how good and great he is; and they tell what he has done; one of the books of the Old Testament*.

punish hurt someone because they have done wrong things.

purple a colour that kings and important people used; like dark red.

ripe fruit or seeds that are ready to eat.

Roman a person or thing from Rome. Rome was a powerful city; it had a strong army.

roots part of plant in the ground.

rope long thin piece of material.

rub move a hand from side to side on a thing.

sacrifice to give something valuable; or, to die for someone, or for God.

Sadducees a group of Jews*. They did not believe that a dead person could become alive again. They only used the first 5 books of the Old Testament*.

salvation make free from evil* and its results.

shake move things to remove the parts that you do not want.

silver valuable metal.

skull bone in head that gives it its shape.

Son of David name for Jesus. Jesus was in the family* of David.

Son of God name for Jesus.

Son of Man a name that Jesus called himself. See Daniel 8:17.

sore place without skin on the body.

special different, better than other people, very great.

spirit a human spirit is the part of a person that is alive, that we cannot see. Our spirit can speak to God and God can speak to our spirit. Bad spirits (also called evil spirits or demons) are spirits that live in the air round us. The devil* is their leader.

spit send water out of the mouth.

sweat water that comes out of the skin.

tears water that comes from the eyes when someone is sad.

tell say what another person must do.

thorn a part of a plant; it is long and sharp.

tongue large red part (of the body) in the mouth.

trust to believe that someone will do the right thing.

vine a plant that has fruit called grapes*. It is a plant that climbs.

vulture large bird that eats dead animals.

way a path to follow, or words to obey.

wheat plant; people make bread with the seeds.

wheels round things that help things like cars to move.

whip thing made out of very long and very thin pieces of material with something sharp tied at the end. People hit a person with it to punish* them.

widow a woman that had a husband that died.

wine a drink that has alcohol in it; people make it from small, sweet fruit called grapes. You can use it as medicine.

wise a wise person understands and does the right thing.

worship to show God that we love him very much.

yeast people put it into flour and water to make bread. It grows in the bread. It causes the bread to rise before you bake it. Jesus used the word to show how people copy each other.

zealot one of a group of people who fought against the Roman* rulers in Israel.